Stories From my grandmother's KITCHEN

a darius williams cookbook

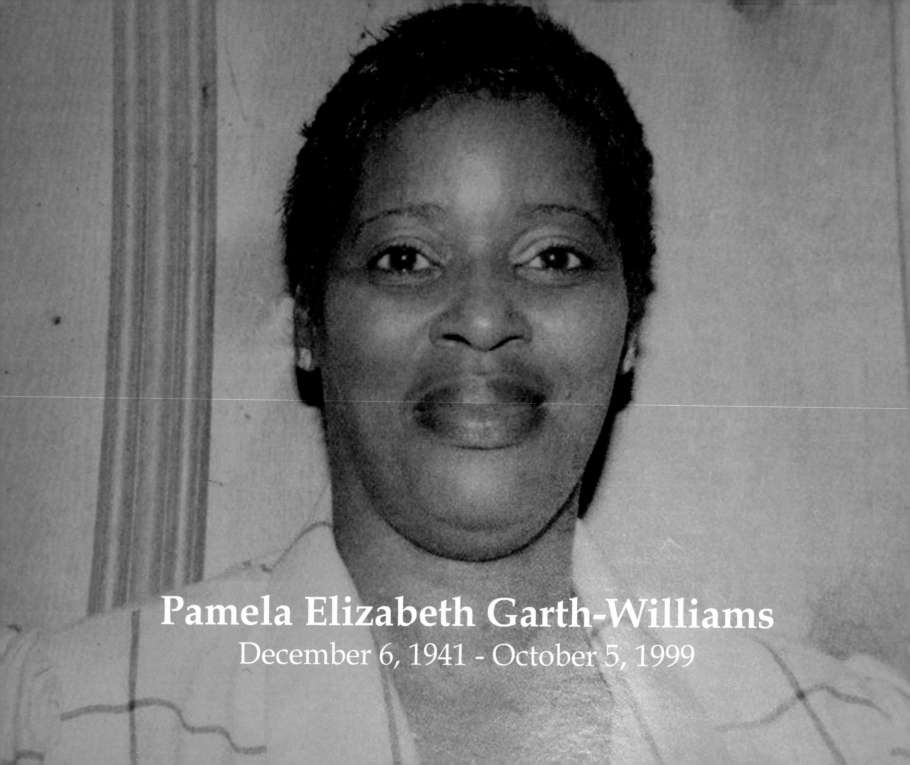

Pamela Elizabeth Garth-Williams
December 6, 1941 - October 5, 1999

a darius williams cookbook

food photography by Darius Williams
model photography by Errol Dunlap

inspired by Pamela Elizabeth Garth

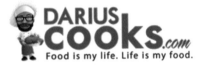

ISBN 978-0-9963478-0-8

Designed by Darius Williams
Typesetting by Darius Williams

introduction

I think it's quite interesting, actually. People look at the types of food I create and ask me, "So, how long have you been cooking?" I never really quite know how to answer that question. I've been enjoying food for a long time now. So, I think a much more appropriate question would center around, "How long have I been eating?" And well, the answer to that is quite simple. I've been eating throughout my entire life. Yes, my entire life I've been enjoying food. It's really been the epicenter of my existence here on Earth. You might laugh, but I'm serious.

I think food has magical abilities. Regardless of who you are, where you've come from, what part of the world broods your ancestral roots, or even your socio-economic status, you've got to eat. Food is really one of the lowest common denominators that connects us all to one another as human beings. That's why I like it so much. In a world full of chaos, craziness, and change, food forces us to stop for a moment and relish in the fact that we're human beings. How this happens and forms into an experience is what really excites me the most.

You could be a financial analyst on Wall Street in New York City taking a bite out of a great deli sandwich during a lunch break on a warm Summer day. Perhaps you're a teacher busy teaching our future leaders and you sit down to eat with a class in the school's cafeteria during your lunch break. Or maybe you're a busy mom who's done all the chores for the day and right before you knock out that next load of laundry, you scramble to get lunch on the table for the little ones. Or, maybe you're able to grab a friend or two and meet up at one of the most amazing brunch spots in your town to laugh, drink, listen and share stories. Regardless of who or where you are, you've got to eat. Remember, it's one of the commonalities that connects us all as human beings. I figured this out a long time ago. Well, sort of. I remember growing up around the holiday times. Life was

good. I had no worries at all - much different than today. My grandmother would start preparation for the big dinners a few days in advance. The moment I would see her light the stove and place the first pot atop the flame, my heart would beat a bit faster and my blood would rush. I mean, I knew that the big dinner was two days away, but it didn't matter. We were officially in preparation mode and that's really all that mattered. It's as if it was game time and we had a goal to meet before the next two days ended. The chopping of vegetables would ensue. The cleaning of meats would begin. And if we were really lucky, there would be some O'jays, Chi-lites, or Temptations playing in the background. That's when you really knew it was game on.

Over the next few days, my grandmother would weave and bend in her kitchen with the precision of a skilled artist. Watching her do this time after time was really the ultimate master class. She would cut and chop and add things to a pot that my young mind could never conceive. To this day, I never remember her using a measuring cup or a measuring spoon. Her tongue was the guide to determine if something needed a dash of this or a pinch of that. Again, I watched in amazement as she worked to get it just right. If it wasn't quite right, she knew just what to do. In the end, I was never really sure of the type of magic she worked, however, dinner went off without a hitch. Roasted meats were always tender and succulent. Dishes with gravies and sauces were savory and herbaceous. Side dishes tasted like the first and third notes of the main dish, creating the perfect harmonies. As we laughed, joked, and told stories, our bellies were filled, one by one. This was our tradition as a family.

Although my grandmother is no longer present with us, her spirit lives on within me. It lives on within our family. It lives on in the food we eat, the stories we tell, the hugs, the laughter, and the jokes. Her spirit is well and alive. It has become my life's mission to bottle the ingredients of my familiar childhood into recipes that welcome present time. This means that I literally take the ingredients that are familiar to me and find brand new ways to present them. I am a believer of pushing the boundaries of creativity. My aim with this book is to put my childhood on a platter, infuse it with a bit of creativity, and provide the blank canvas to create many more memories for the world to enjoy.

Let me list a few disclaimers. I do have a cooking philosophy. I think food should always be simple, easy, and delicious. You will not find recipes in the book that take forever to cook or recipes that have a ton of steps. It's something I just don't believe in. I do believe those laborious recipes are necessary. However, when my tummy is growling, I prefer to satisfy my cravings really quickly. You should also know that there aren't a lot of steps to these recipes. There are some foundational methods that you will probably learn, if you don't already know them. For example, I start my mac and cheese recipes off with a classic white sauce called a béchamel. The start of a béchamel requires making a roux. A roux is a thickening agent used to tighten up sauces, gravies, and stews. Don't let that intimidate you. It's a fancy word, but all you do is stir together butter and flour for a few minutes over a medium flame. See? It's super simple.

You'll also find a few whimsical recipes. That's one of the reasons I wrote this book. Chicken is a blank canvas. There are literally millions of recipes for chicken. I wanted to stretch the boundaries and figure out how to present chicken in new ways. So, my chicken meatloaf with sweet red sauce is one of them. Also, my collard green and cornbread cake is is topped with some delectable fried chicken. I also think my lime and garlic chicken with capers recipe is a really great twist on the classic Italian recipe for scampi. See what I mean? Food should be fun. And it shouldn't take all day to get to the fun, either.

If you've followed me for any period of time on social media, you should know that I post tons of recipes to my food blog - http://www.DariusCooks.com. If you've seen these recipes or tried a few, you know they're super easy because I don't use a lot of fussy ingredients. I am a believer in staples. This is how you turn out a meal. You should have the staples ready to rock and roll. If you peruse my cupboards, you'll see some pretty basic ingredients. I use really simple things like cumin, Kosher salt, a good chili powder, granulated garlic, Sazon, onion powder, fresh ground black pepper, Hungarian paprika, dried Italian herbs, white and brown sugars, and red chili flakes. I always keep some citrus on hand; by me, you can get 8 limes for about a dollar. I always pick up some when I'm at the market. My other staples are things like balsamic vinegar, rice wine vinegar, good olive oil, and some type of vegetable or canola oil. That's pretty much it. Pretty basic, right?

When it comes to produce, I always buy fresh. I make a few exceptions for things that freeze really well. I think peas, corn kernels, and green beans are great frozen. Other than that, everything else is bought fresh, especially if it's in season. When it comes to canned produce, I typically only buy beans (which I rinse well to get rid of that horrible canning liquid), tomatoes, olives, and artichokes. Again, everything else has to be fresh. The recipes just work out better that way. I typically always buy and cook with fresh fruit. However, in a pinch, I'll use frozen stone fruit or berries for a cobbler or chutney. You don't have to follow my rules. Create your own. It's more fun when you figure out what works for you and your palate.

I hope as you read and create from this cookbook, you enjoy it as much as I have. I hope your inspiration runs wild and you create countless memories just like I have. Let these recipes serve as the canvas. Allow your personality, culinary climate, family, and passion be the colors that turn the blank canvas into a masterpiece. The world needs to see! And listen, if you do make any of the recipes from this book, I'll personally shout you out on Instagram. So, be sure to tag me when you post the picture (@DariusCooks). Yes, this is my own little plot to make everyone jealous who isn't enjoying the delicious eats from this book. I'm grateful for your interest in my recipes and I'm humbled that you're allowing me into your kitchen. Remember, there's much more at my website - it's DariusCooks.com. Let me leave you with these last two thoughts: Food is my life. Life is my food. I wish you happy cooking from my heart to yours!

table of contents

Appetizers Snacks & Whatnots

16 - Crispy Pork Belly with Whipped Feta & Green Apple Salsa

18 - Chicken & Waffle Fritters

21 - Crispy Grilled Cheese Wont-tons

28 - Chicken & Biscuits on a Stick with Sausage & Herb Gravy

31 - Cornbread Cupcakes with Mashed Potato Frosting

33 - Cranberry Orange Relish

35 - Collard Green & Artichoke Fondue

37 - Chicken Meatballs with Sweet Red Sauce

39 - Prosciutto Wrapped Asparagus with Balsamic Glaze

41 - Spinach & Artichoke Stuffed Shrimp

43 - Mini Ham, Cheese, and Potato Tarts

46 - Butter Pecan Cornbread with Honey Butter

48 - Scampi Grilled Chicken Bites

50 - French Fry Crusted Chicken Strips

Salads, Soups, & Stews

55 - Southern Style Potato Salad

57 - New Orleans Style Red Beans & Rice

59 - Chicken & Waffle Caesar Salad

61 - Pea & Cheddar Salad with Cajun Grilled Shrimp

63 - English Cucumber Salad with Balsamic Dressing

65 - Slow Cooker Short Rib & Sweet Potato Stew

Side Dishes

70 - Spicy Braised Collard Greens with Smoked Turkey

72 - Grandma Pam's Fried Sweet Corn

74 - Spinach & Artichoke Risotto

77 - Crispy Okra with Chili-Lime Salt

80 - Roasted Potatoes with Dill Chimichurri

82 - Coconut Yam Rice

85 - Sautéed Green Beans with Crispy Potatoes

87 - Chili Garlic Cabbage

89 - Grilled Corn on the Cob with Honey Butter

91 - Spinach & Artichoke Twice Baked Potatoes

93 - White Cheddar & Garlic Scalloped Potatoes

97 - Winter Succotash with Bacon

100 - Collard Green Pesto Roasted Tomatoes

102 - Balsamic & Honey Roasted Brussels Sprouts

105 - Stewed Greens & Tomatoes

109 - The Ultimate Baked Mac & Cheese

111 - Whipped Sweet Potatoes with Salt

113 - Creamed Field Greens with French Fried Onions

115 - Roasted Veggie Rice Pilaf

117 - Southern Style Sausage & Cornbread Dressing

Main Dishes, Meats, & Seafoods

121 - Peach Balsamic Glazed Wings

123 - Sriracha Glazed Chicken Wings

125 - Crispy Chicken with Lime Caper Sauce

127 - Garlic & Herb Roast Chicken with Roasted Root Vegetables

130 - Chicken Fried Shrimp with Corn & Bacon Gravy

133 - Jerk Fried Chicken

135 - Chicken Sausage Breakfast Hash-lettes

137 - Double Cheddar Ox-Tail Sandwich with Sweet Lime Slaw

139 - Lemon & Garlic Pork Chops

141 - Shrimp & Grits with Bacon Butter

143 - My Granny's Brown Bag Fried Chicken

Desserts and All Things Sweet

appetizers, snacks, and whatnots

CRISPY PORK BELLY *with whipped feta & green apple salsa*

yield: *Makes 8 servings* | prep time: *15 minutes* | cook time: *2 hours, 15 minutes*

Ingredients

For the braised pork belly
-2 pounds of pork belly
-1 teaspoon of Kosher salt
-1 teaspoon of black pepper
-4 garlic cloves
-1 small onion, diced
-3 bay leaves
-1 teaspoon of fresh oregano
-1 cup of chicken stock
-1 cup of good white wine

-1 cup of flour
-1/2 cup of corn starch
-3-4 cups of Canola oil

For the whipped feta
-8 ounces of feta cheese
-2 garlic cloves
-3/4 cup of heavy cream
-1/2 teaspoon of black pepper

For the green apple salsa
-2 cups of diced green apple
-2 garlic cloves, minced
-1 tablespoon of minced jalapeño
-1 tablespoon of chopped cilantro
-1 tablespoon of olive oil
-1 tablespoon of lime juice
-1 teaspoon of sugar
-1/2 teaspoon of Kosher salt
-1/2 teaspoon of black pepper

-Toast, for serving

"Don't stress over this recipe. Make the pork belly a day or two ahead of time. Then, when you're ready for it, slice it and fry it up. It cuts easier after it has chilled."

-Grandma Pam

1. Preheat the oven to 350 degrees. Add all the ingredients for the braised pork belly in an oven safe dish, seal tightly with aluminum foil, and cook for 2 hours until the pork belly is tender.

2. In a large bowl, mix together the flour and cornstarch. Once the pork belly has cooled, slice into 2-inch pieces and toss in the flour and cornstarch mixture.

3. Preheat the Canola oil to 360 degrees and then fry the pork belly on both sides until crispy.

4. To make the whipped feta, put all the ingredients into a food processor and blend until smooth. Keep chilled until you're ready to use it.

5. To make the green apple salsa, combine all ingredients into a bowl and mix well. Keep refrigerated until you're ready to use it. To assemble, spread some whipped feta over the toast. Then top each piece with crispy pork belly and green apple salsa.

NOTE: If you're a pork belly novice, then be aware. Pork belly can be super fatty. Either have your butcher trim some down for you or look for a few meaty pieces yourself.

CHICKEN & WAFFLE *fritters*

yield: *Makes 4 servings* | prep time: *15 minutes* | cook time: *25 minutes*

Ingredients

Chicken Sausage Nuggets
-1 pound of ground chicken
-2 teaspoons of brown sugar
-1 teaspoon of Kosher salt
-1 teaspoon of ground black pepper
-1/2 teaspoon of dried sage
-1/2 teaspoon of dried oregano
-1/2 teaspoon of chili powder

Waffle Batter
-2 eggs
-2 cups of all purpose flour
-1 3/4 cups of milk
-1/2 cup of vegetable oil
-1 teaspoon of white sugar
-4 teaspoons of baking powder
-1/4 teaspoon of salt
-1/2 teaspoon vanilla extract

-12 toothpicks
-4 cups of vegetable or canola oil, for frying
-Powdered sugar, for garnishing
-Maple syrup, for dipping

"Keep this sausage recipe handy. It works with any type of ground meat. It's the go-to sausage for breakfasts and brunches!"

—Grandma Pam

1. To make the sausage, preheat the oven to 375 degrees.
2. Add the chicken, brown sugar, salt, black pepper, dried sage, dried oregano, and chili powder to a bowl and mix well to combine.
3. Form into 12 1-inch balls and arrange on a sheet tray lined with parchment paper. Roast in the oven for 8-12 minutes, or until cooked through.
4. Meanwhile, preheat cooking oil to 360° F.
5. In a large bowl, combine the flour, sugar, baking powder, and salt. Mix well.
6. Then, add in the eggs, milk, vanilla extract, and vegetable oil. Mix well to combine.
7. Using a toothpick, grab a cooked chicken sausage nugget and dunk it in the waffle batter. Then, fry them up until they're golden brown on the outside and light and fluffy on the inside. Drain on paper towels and garnish with powdered sugar and maple syrup.

NOTE: Be sure the oil isn't too hot. The last thing you want to do is to have the outside of the fritters golden brown while the insides are still raw.

My Granny & Pancakes

Let's face it. I loved my Granny. I did. She was kind and sweet. She was nurturing and loving. She was one of the best cooks I know. No one, and I do mean no one, could rock a pleated skirt from "Ward's" and a white blouse from "Penney's" quite like my Granny. That was her signature outfit. She'd add a pearl or two. Then, she'd spray some Aquanet in her hair. The moment she dabbed on some White Diamonds perfume, you could tell her nothing. You couldn't tell Pamela Elizabeth Garth-Williams that she wasn't sharp. In all of her amazement, one thing puzzled me. I never knew why Granny couldn't make pancakes from scratch. She tried once. She did. I ate part of it to be nice. I had been to pancake houses as a kid, so I knew how pancakes were supposed to taste.

My local church also operated a Christian school that I attended until 2nd grade. There was a bus that would pick us up in the morning. However, it wasn't a regular school bus. It was a huge coach bus the church also used for our church trips. The bus driver was Mr. Parker. He used to drive that huge bus and he'd pick me up early in the morning along the student pick-up route. He'd pick me up first and we'd park right outside of the McDonald's that used to be near Madison & Pulaski on the west side of Chicago. This was a morning ritual.

My order was always the same, hot cakes and sausage. Back then, it was only about a dollar. So, I knew how pancakes were supposed to be when they were done right. They were lightly golden brown. They were soft to the touch and the insides were fluffy like freshly folded laundry. The sweet cream butter was pure. If you tasted it and licked your lips the right way, you'd get a little hint of salty pure goodness on your tongue. As you pulled back the plastic on the container and revealed the butter, it would have melted slightly. You'd take your knife and scrape out the contents, then you'd smear the butter on the hot pancakes and watch the butter immediately melt into the pancakes like a summer sun falling behind the horizon. The best part was the syrup. It had a real maple taste to it and as you poured it over the pancakes, it would fall down the sides of the pancakes like the fresh dew falling from a brisk morning's leaf. As you cut into the pancakes, the gooey syrup and butter oozes out a bit more, but you manage to collect it on your fork. One taste and you knew that life couldn't get any better than it had at that moment. Although it was a pancake with butter and syrup, the combination was so harmonious that it made life make sense.

CRISPY GRILLED *cheese won-tons*

Ingredients

- 12 won-ton wrappers
- 12 mozzarella string cheese sticks
- a bowl of water

- 4-6 cups of vegetable or canola oil, for frying.

"Won-ton wrappers have a tendency to dry out pretty quickly. So, have your assembly line set up and ready to go!"
—Grandma Pam

1. Take all of the string cheese out of the wrappers and cut them in half.
2. Stuff two pieces of cheese in the center of the won-ton. Then, using the diagram on the packaging, roll each won-ton tightly.
3. Dab your fingers in water and run them across the edge of the won-ton wrapper. Be gentle and press firmly to seal each won-ton wrapper closed.
4. Place the won-tons in the fridge for at least 20-30 minutes so that they dry out a bit. This ensures they'll stay sealed when cooking.
5. When you're ready, preheat the oil to 360° F. When the oil is hot, fry each won-ton until it's golden brown. Drain the excess oil on paper towels and enjoy the crispy grilled cheese won-tons while they're still hot.

NOTE: When frying anything, never over-crowd the pan. If need be, cook in batches. This is your insurance policy that the oil stays hot enough to ensure each won-ton comes out crispy and not logged with oil.

Ms. Robinson's Cheese Toast

I think it's pretty funny that I grew up a church kid. I love church. I think I love it more for the social aspect more than anything else. We grew up with such a small biological family, so our church family was such a huge extension of just about everything we did. As a kid, I had so many people watching out for me. They were the eyes and ears that kept my deviant self in check when my grandmother wasn't around.

I went to a private school that was run by my church for elementary school. The lines between Sunday service and weekday school were blurred because I saw the same people all the time. It was just that on Sundays, they were dressed to the nines. Back then, you really got dressed up for church. Ms. Robinson was always decked out in her best white dresses and hats. Yes, she could wear a hat. She had the silkiest gray hair. I always remembered her that way. From the time I was a kid until I was an adult, she always looked the same. She didn't age. She didn't get older. She didn't get younger. She just seemed to always be the same, kind and sweet and always with a smile. She wasn't just the church mother, but she was also the lunch lady at our school. She prepared all of our meals. Just about every morning, she would make this cheese toast concoction. If I tried, I'm sure I could never get it just quite like she did. I think it was nothing more than buttered toast with cheese.

We had an Aldi grocery store down the street from the school. Some mornings, she'd go down there and pick up the ingredients and then bring them back to the school to prepare them. She'd cut slices from the brick of cheese. Then, she'd melt butter. As best I can remember, she'd brush each slice of white bread with butter before she topped them with cheese. Then, she'd put the tray of buttered bread and cheese into the oven to toast. What I tasted was downright amazing. Although simple in composition, it was extremely complex in experience. It really was the right amount of saltiness from the cheese and butter to let your taste buds know something was going on. There was this crunch from the toast. It wasn't too crunchy because there was still this soft characteristic that was left toward the middle of each slice of bread. It was almost intentional, parable-like even. Then, the cheese would ooze perfectly as you bit into it because she removed it from the oven just at the right time. The warm cheese had nowhere to go, so it would fall from the sides of your mouth as you bit into the toast. Instinctively, each reaction was the same. You'd take your index finger, grab the warm melted cheese, and plop it in your mouth. It was a shame to let things like this go to waste. If you ate it right, you'd have a wad of cheese and bread stuck inside your mouth. You know, back between your gums and your teeth. No matter your level of sophistication or socio-economic status, you knew better. You'd reach your finger back there, pull that gooey deliciousness to the front of your mouth, sit back, and let the residue of the experience slide down your throat to your tummy. This was surely a bite of heaven, pun intended.

Popping Biscuits...and Smiles!

I don't think it was until I got older that I realized that another way actually existed. For me, every Saturday night with Granny was the same routine. It really was the pre-game for Sunday morning. After a day full of chores and errands, it was time to start the ritual. That meant you had to get your church clothes out and ironed. In Granny's household, ironing on a Sunday would get you drop kicked. It's something you just didn't do. Besides having your clothes ready, you had to read your Sunday school lesson for the week along with memorizing the Golden Text. We had Sunday school book. They came out every quarter like clockwork. On the front cover of the book would be a beautiful church somewhere in rural America. There was enough material in there to last three whole months and you had to study it Saturday before going to bed. After reading my lesson and memorizing my scripture, I would secretly indulge with my grandmother. She absolutely loved watching two TV shows, Walker Texas Ranger and Mama's Family. To this day, my love for Mama's Family is because we used to watch it together each Saturday night. I think somewhere between that and the Hoosier Lottery game show, I'd drift off and fall asleep.

When I woke up the next morning, it was to the aroma of whichever flowery fragrance my grandmother was wearing that Sunday mixed with something cooking in the kitchen. We were (and still are) bacon people. It was nothing for me to smell bacon crisping up in some cast iron skillet on top of the stove. Somewhere between me folding up my blanket and getting out of the shower, I would see my grandmother grab a can of those biscuits. You know, the kind that you unwrap and then would need to hit against the counter so that they could bust open. She would hit the package against the counter, lay the biscuits out on a sheet tray, and bake them up until they were golden brown and flaky. For some reason, etched in my brain is my grandmother, fresh with rollers in her hair and half dressed in a white lace slip, with one hand on her hip, hitting the can of biscuits against the counter until it popped open.

I'm sure I was about 10 or 11. Or, maybe it was 11 or 12. I can't remember the exact age, but I'll never forget the experience. Growing up, every 3rd Sunday of the month was Youth Sunday at our local church. This was something to look forward to because this meant that everything the adults typically did, us kids got a chance to do. We would sing in the choir. We would usher. We would do some sort of public speaking. If you were lucky, then you'd help out in the kitchen.

There's no need to wonder where I was. I did my fair share of ushering and singing in the choir, but I loved being in the kitchen helping prepare breakfast for the parishioners. At the time, I was a young lad and very inexperienced. I wasn't supposed to know how to do much in the kitchen and come to think of it, I didn't. I've always been a natural observer. I do remember watching the ladies move about the kitchen with the elegance of a graceful swan doing its farewell dance.

They'd know how to cut the onion just right. They'd know just how much seasoning to add to this pot or that pan. They'd even know how many stirs the contents of a pot would get. They worked as though they were looking for a certain texture or consistency, then they'd stop and go on to the next task. It's as if they were confident that they had done all they could've so that the food was perfect. There were about 5 or 6 women in the kitchen and although no one said a word, they moved about with harmony and grace. There would be a huge selection of things to choose from; grits, sausage, bacon, toast, hash browns, rice, and even biscuits. You name it and it was usually there.

Ms. Adams is her name. She is one of my biggest cooking inspirations. She cooked and it was good. Period. She also had this super commanding presence that made you want to just do what she said because you instinctively felt it was the right thing to do. She would say, "Darius, go put the orange juice on the tables." I did as she said. Then, I felt such an overwhelming sense of accomplishment as I looked and saw the juice sitting on the tables. Yes, I did that. I was proud. One of the last things I would see her do before breakfast was served was to put a pan of biscuits in the oven. As I arranged my orange juice on the tables just right, I would hear that familiar bang. I moved from one table to the next making sure the juice was set up just right. I would look over at Ms. Adams and see her bang that can of biscuits against the edge of the counter until it popped. Ironically, she had one hand on her hip as she popped open each can of biscuits. I took notice of the moment and smiled inside myself. As I made sure the orange juice was properly placed on the next table, I put that "one hand on the hip, beat the can against the edge of the counter" technique in my memory banks. I don't know how I knew to do that; I just did. Every time I open a can of biscuits, I can smell my grandmother's Sunday morning perfume, bacon crisping in the pan, and I still smile inside myself.

CHICKEN & BISCUITS *on a stick with sausage & herb gravy*

yield: *Makes 6 servings* | prep time: *15 minutes* | cook time: *30 minutes*

Ingredients

For the fried chicken

-2 large chicken breasts, boneless & skinless, cut into about 2 inch cubes
-1 teaspoon of salt
-1 teaspoon of pepper
-1/2 teaspoon of granulated garlic
-2 cups of flour
-1 cup of cornstarch
-1 egg, beaten with about a tablespoon of water

-1 can of refrigerator biscuits
-skewers
-oil for frying

For the gravy

-1 pound of sausage
-1 tablespoon of minced garlic
-1/4 cup of minced onion
-2 tablespoons of butter
-2 tablespoons of flour
-2 cups of half and half
-a few sprigs of fresh thyme
-1 tablespoon of ground black pepper
-1 teaspoon of salt, to taste

"This is my go-to recipe for a party. You can keep the skewers in a warm oven until you're ready to serve and you can keep the gravy warm in a slow cooker. It works every time!"

—Grandma Pam

1. Preheat the oven to 350 degrees. Cut the biscuits into 4 equal pieces and bake them in the oven until they're golden brown.

2. Meanwhile, preheat the oil for frying the chicken. To season the chicken, toss it in a bowl with salt, pepper, and garlic powder. Then, toss the chicken in the egg wash mixture and then dredge in a bowl mixed with the flour and cornstarch. Shake off the excess flour and fry the chicken pieces until they're golden brown.

3. To make the gravy, cook the sausage, garlic, and onion together in the butter until the sausage is just cooked through. Add in the fresh thyme and flour and cook for about 60 seconds while constantly stirring.

4. Add in the half and half, being sure to scrape the bottom of the pan. Once the mixture comes to a boil, it will thicken. Season with salt and pepper.

5. To serve, thread the chicken and biscuits on a skewer and serve with a heaping amount of sausage & herb gravy for dipping.

NOTE: If you want to get the biscuits perfectly round, use a mini-biscuit or cookie cutter. Then, bake the biscuits. They'll come out uniform and make your presentation awesome!

CORNBREAD CUPCAKES *with mashed potato frosting*

ield: *Makes 6 servings* | prep time: *30 minutes* | cook time: *45 minutes*

Ingredients

Cornbread Cupcakes
-1 cup of all purpose flour
-1 cup of cornmeal
-1 cup of sugar
-1 stick of melted butter
-2 eggs
-2 teaspoons of baking powder
-1 teaspoon of salt
-about 1 1/2 cups of buttermilk

Mashed Potato Frosting
-2 pounds of potatoes, boiled, drained and cooled
-1 stick of room temperature butter
-1 tablespoon of salt
-1 tablespoon of black pepper
-1/2 tablespoon of granulated garlic
-1/3 cup of half and half

-Fried chicken, to garnish
-Your favorite hot sauce, to garnish

"Keep the ingredients on hand for the cornbread. It's my go-to recipe for cornbread and it ALWAYS turns out perfect. No more blue box cornbread!"

-Grandma Pam

1. Preheat the oven to 375 degrees.

2. In a large bowl, just dump all the ingredients for the cornbread cupcakes into a bowl and mix until smooth. Pour into cupcake liners and bake until golden brown. This should take about 9-12 minutes. Then, take them out to cool.

3. Meanwhile, to make the mashed potatoes, heat the half and half and butter on the stove until it's hot, but not boiling.

4. Mash in the potatoes until they're smooth. Then, season with salt, pepper, and granulated garlic. Be sure to stir in the seasonings well so they're distributed evenly.

5. Using a pastry bag, pipe on the mashed potatoes on each cupcake. Then, top with fried chicken and a dash of hot sauce

NOTE: This idea is perfect for a party. Another super cute idea is to make mini cornbread muffins and top them with a dollop of mashed potatoes and fried chicken. If you don't have a pastry bag, no worries. Grab a spoon or a butter knife and just pile some on. There's no wrong way to do this.

CRANBERRY & orange relish

Ingredients

- 3 cups of fresh cranberries
- 1 cup of fresh squeezed orange juice
- 3/4 cup of sugar
- 1/2 teaspoon of salt
- zest of 1 orange

"With a few simple ingredients, you can put that canned cranberry crap to rest. Besides, this version tastes much better!"
—Grandma Pam

1. In a sauce pan, cook the cranberries, sugar, and orange juice until the cranberries have started to pop open. This takes about 7-8 minutes.
2. Then, stir the salt and orange zest.
3. Remove from the heat, place the relish into a bowl and refrigerate until you're ready to use.

NOTE: Experiment with the flavors! Tequila and lime, whiskey and cherry, or even pineapple and coconut are great additions to add to your cranberry relish. The sky is the limit!

COLLARD GREEN & *artichoke fondue*

Ingredients

- 2 tablespoons of butter
- 2 tablespoons of flour
- 1 cup of whole milk
- 1 1/2 cups of half and half
- 1 teaspoon of salt
- 1 tablespoon of black pepper
- 1/2 tablespoon of garlic powder
- 2 cups of shredded white cheddar cheese
- 1 cup of chopped collard greens, frozen, thawed, and drained
- 1 cup of diced artichoke hearts

- pita chips or crostini, for serving

"Frozen collard greens are perfect for this recipe. But, if you can't find the frozen kind, try frozen spinach or sautéed kale. Whatever you do, just drain the greens really well before adding them to the sauce."

—Grandma Pam

1. In a large pot, on high heat, melt the butter and then sprinkle in the flour. Stir often and cook until the mixture turns a light golden brown - about 2 minutes.

2. Then, whisk in the milk and half and half. Continue to stir until the mixture begins to thicken, then reduce the heat.

3. Season the sauce with salt, pepper, and garlic powder. Also, add the white cheddar cheese, collard greens, and artichoke hearts.

4. Continuing to stir, cook the fondue until it's thick. Serve with crostini or pita chips.

NOTE: If you don't have wooden spoon, this is a great time to invest in one. A wooden spoon is great for stirring the contents of the pot without damaging the pan. It's just perfect for this recipe.

field: *Makes 8 servings* | prep time: *10 minutes* | cook time: *15 minutes*

Ingredients

-2 pounds of ground chicken
-3 slices of white bread (crust removed)
-1 cup of buttermilk
-1/2 cup of grated onion
-3 cloves of minced garlic
-1/2 cup of grated green bell pepper
-1/2 cup of grated celery
-1 tablespoon of salt
-1 tablespoon of pepper
-1/2 tablespoon of onion powder
-3 tablespoons of olive oil
-1/2 tablespoon of paprika
-1 pinch of chili flakes

For the sweet red sauce
-2 cups of canned crushed tomatoes
-2 tablespoons of sugar
-a pinch of salt

"The key to making these meatballs is simple. Use a sheet tray. The low sides of the sheet tray allow the heat to hit the meatballs on all sides ensuring the outside gets sort of crispy while the inside stays nice and moist."

-Grandma Pam

1. Preheat the oven to 375 degrees. Also, add the bread to a bowl and pour in the buttermilk to soften to bread.

2. Meanwhile, in a large bowl, combine the ground chicken, onion, garlic, bell pepper, celery, salt, pepper, onion powder, paprika, olive oil and chili flakes. Mix well and then add the softened bread. You can discard any buttermilk that didn't get absorbed in the bread.

3. Form the meatballs into 1 inch round balls and then arrange on a sheet tray. Bake in the oven for 10-12 minutes until the meatballs are cooked through.

4. For the sauce, add the tomatoes, sugar, and salt to a sauce pot. Cook on medium heat for 6-8 minutes until the sauce is warmed throughout.

5. To serve, pour the sauce over the meatballs and garnish with fresh herbs.

NOTE: When you buy ground chicken, be careful. There's the kind that's ground with all white meat from the breast. Then, there's the kind that ground from the breast and thigh. The latter is so much more flavorful!

PROSCIUTTO WRAPPED *asparagus with balsamic glaze*

yield: *Makes 4 servings* | prep time: *10 minutes* | cook time: *15 minutes*

Ingredients

- 1 cup of balsamic vinegar
- 16 stalks of asparagus
- 16 slices of prosciutto

"This recipe is so simple, it shouldn't qualify as a recipe. But, it's also fancy. It's one of those recipes that takes seconds to put together and people will think you spent all day working on it."

—Grandma Pam

1. In a sauce pan, add the balsamic vinegar and cook on medium heat until the vinegar has thickened. Then, remove from the heat and let cool.

2. Meanwhile, preheat the oven to 400 degrees.

3. Clip the ends of each piece of asparagus, being sure to get rid of the woodsy part towards the bottom of the stalk. Then, wrap each piece of asparagus with a slice of prosciutto.

4. Place the asparagus on a sheet tray and roast for 4-5 minutes, until the prosciutto are crispy. Drizzle with balsamic glaze and enjoy.

NOTE: Be sure to watch the glaze. It can go from thick and perfect to burned and bitter in a matter of seconds. Also, be sure to keep a window open or turn on the exhaust. The smell of vinegar cooking can be powerful. But it tastes so good!

PINACH & ARTICHOKE *stuffed shrimp*

Ingredients

For the filling
- 4 ounces of cream cheese, room temperature
- 1 cup of frozen spinach, drained
- 1/2 cup of finely diced artichoke hearts
- 1/2 teaspoon of salt
- 1/2 teaspoon of pepper
- 1/2 cup of grated Parmesan cheese
- 1/2 tablespoon of garlic powder
- 1 pound of jumbo shrimp, cleaned and deveined

For the topping
- 2 cups of Panko breadcrumbs
- 2 tablespoons of melted butter
- 2 tablespoons of fresh parsley, chopped

"If you're like me, then shrimp is usually reserved for a special occasion. But, the flavor profile works wonders. So, use this same process for fish, chicken, or even pork chops!"

—Grandma Pam

1. Preheat the oven to 375 degrees. In a large bowl, mix together all the ingredients for the filling.
2. Cut the shrimp deeply lengthwise, but don't cut through the shrimp completely. The shrimp should still be in one piece.
3. Stuff as much filling as desired in each shrimp. Meanwhile, mix together the breadcrumbs, melted butter, and chopped parsley in a separate bowl.
4. Top each shrimp with the breadcrumb mixture and arrange on a sheet tray. Roast the shrimp until the topping is golden brown and the shrimp have cooked through. Serve warm.

NOTE: Be sure never to overcook the shrimp. A rule of thumb is to always take the shrimp out when they're just barely cooked. The heat from the pan will allow for carry over cooking. This way, the shrimp will be perfect and juicy!

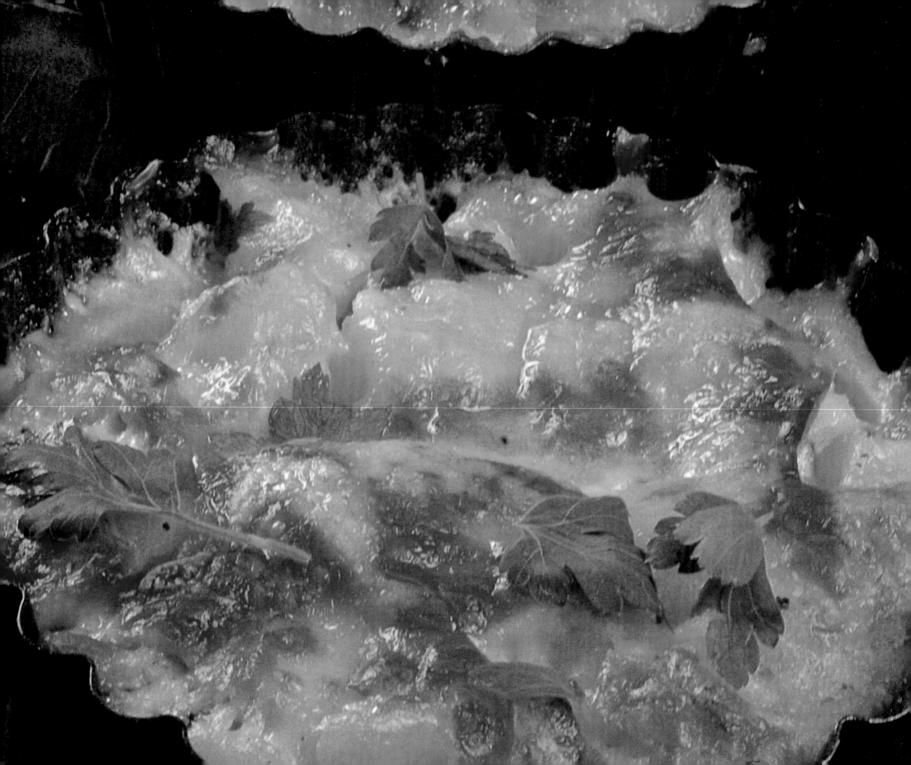

MINI HAM, CHEESE, and potato tarts

Yield: Makes 4 servings | prep time: 10 minutes | cook time: 25 minutes

Ingredients

- 4 Yukon gold potatoes
- 3 cloves of garlic
- 1 teaspoon of salt
- 1 teaspoon of white pepper
- 4 tablespoons of room temperature butter
- about 1/4 cup of half and half
- 1 cup of shredded white cheddar
- 1 cup of diced ham
- 1/2 cup of shredded white cheddar, for topping
- cilantro, to garnish

"This recipe is great for brunch or cleaning out your fridge. You can use any meats or veggies you've got laying around to add to the filling for this recipe!"

—Grandma Pam

1. Start by dicing the potatoes in chunks, then boil in water with garlic cloves until fork tender. Preheat the oven to 400 degrees.
2. Drain the potatoes well, then add salt, pepper, butter, half and half, shredded white cheddar, and ham. Stir well to combine.
3. Using 4 mini-tart pans, evenly distribute the filling. Then top each one with cheese and bake in the oven for about 12 minutes or until golden brown.
4. Top each tart with cilantro leaves and serve warm.

NOTE: This recipe specifically calls for Yukon gold potatoes because they're super buttery and creamy. But, don't stress if you can't find them. Just use whatever potatoes you have handy. The dish will still come out great!

The #307 Pace Bus

If we were lucky, and it was a nice day out, about once a month my Grandmother and I would go to the shopping center. It was an experience because, although my grandmother didn't have much money, she knew just what she needed in order to stay fly. She was a lover of a pleated skirt. That was her style. A white or pastel colored blouse was what you could find her wearing the most. When it was time to go shopping for Easter or a church service, we would get up early Saturday morning and head out to the shopping center. It was a great time between just she and I. As we walked down the street, I could see her calculating just what she was going to purchase. My grandmother wasn't an impulse buyer. When you come from as little as we had, you can't afford to impulse buy. We would walk to the "El." That's short for the elevated train in Chicago. We'd catch the Green Line from our stop at Austin over through Oak Park to a stop called Harlem. Then, we had to catch a bus. While we were waiting on the bus, I'd look around and take in the sights. It's long gone now, but there used to be an Arby's on the corner of Harlem & Lake across from the bus stop. There was also a Dunkin Donuts there. I'd stand amongst the people waiting on the bus trying to look important. Besides, I was the man of my family going shopping with my grandmother. It was my duty.

We would catch the #307 Pace bus that would take us right to North Riverside Shopping Center. It's the mall, but my grandmother couldn't let certain words go from her youth. It was always an icebox instead of a refrigerator. She'd always say, "give me just a lil' taste" instead of just asking for a small portion. It would always be shopping center, not the mall. We never really made it through the entire shopping center. My Granny didn't have time for that. Instead, we went to one of her two absolute favorite stores Penney's or Ward's. She absolutely loved those stores. To this day, I'll never know why. But that was really the only part of the shopping center we visited. Every once in a while, we'd stop at the Walgreens. My granny had to pick up a few items. One would be some of that green rubbing alcohol. She loved that stuff. Then, she'd always pick up a pack of panty hose. I remember her specifically buying nude and coffee. I didn't know what nude even was back then, I just know that was her favorite. She would always stop for a pack of ice cream too. She loved butter pecan flavored ice cream. That's what we'd do. We'd wait in the hot sun on Harlem Ave. for the #307 Pace bus to go back home. I always had a cone with cookie dough and she always had a cone with butter pecan.

BUTTER PECAN CORNBREAD *with honey butter*

yield: *Makes 8 servings* | prep time: *10 minutes* | cook time: *35 minutes*

Ingredients

-1 cup of corn meal
-1 cup of flour
-1 cup of sugar
-2 eggs
-1 stick of butter, melted
-1 teaspoon of salt
-2 tablespoons of baking powder
-1 cup of frozen corn kernels
-3/4 cup of chopped pecans
-1 1/4 cup of buttermilk

For the honey butter
-1 stick of butter, room temperature
-2 tablespoons of honey
-1 pinch of salt

"I always used the blue box to make cornbread. One taste with this recipe and you'll never use the blue box again!"

-Grandma Pam

1. Preheat the oven to 375 degrees.

2. In a large bowl, mix together together the corn meal, flour, sugar, salt, and baking powder until well combined. Then, add the eggs, melted butter, and buttermilk. Mix until smooth. Then, fold in the corn kernels and chopped pecans.

3. Pour the cornbread in an oven safe dish that's been buttered and bake until the cornbread is golden brown.

4. Meanwhile, to make the honey butter, just mix together the butter, honey, and a pinch of salt in a bowl until well combined.

5. When the cornbread is done, remove from the oven and slather the honey butter over the top of the cornbread.

> **NOTE:** Adding corn to this recipe is a genius idea. However, only use frozen or fresh corn kernels. Canned corn has way too much liquid and will ruin the batter. Creamed corn is the same way. It contains too much liquid and will ruin the final product.

SCAMPI GRILLED *chicken bites*

yield: *Makes 4 servings* | prep time: *5 minutes* | cook time: *20 minutes*

Ingredients

-2 large chicken breasts, boneless and skinless, cut into bite sized pieces
-2 tablespoons of olive oil
-2 tablespoons of butter
-1/2 teaspoon of salt
-1 teaspoon of pepper
-1 cup of good white wine
-1/4 cup of fresh squeezed lemon juice
-3 cloves of garlic, minced
-1/4 cup of chopped parsley

"This is the perfect quick cooking meal. In about 15 minutes, this dish will be done. Pair it with crusty bread, for dipping, and a side salad and you'll be super satisfied!"

-Grandma Pam

1. Sauté the chicken in olive oil until just cooked through. Then, season with salt and pepper.
2. Add the garlic to the pan and let cook for about 30 seconds before adding the white wine. Allow the white wine to reduce. Be sure to scrape the bits off the bottom of the pan while the white wine cooks down.
3. After the white wine has reduced by half, add the lemon juice, butter, and parsley. Stir to combine and cook for another 2-3 minutes. Serve while hot.

NOTE: This recipe calls for using a good white wine. A nice $9 bottle of Chardonnay, Pino Grigio, or Sauvignon Blanc will work just fine. Don't break the bank. If you're going to cook with it, just choose something that you'd also drink.

FRENCH FRY CRUSTED *chicken strips*

yield: *Makes 4 servings* | prep time: *10 minutes* | cook time: *15 minutes*

Ingredients

-2 chicken breasts, boneless and skinless, cut into strips
-1 teaspoon of salt
-1 teaspoon of black pepper
-1 teaspoon of garlic powder
-2 cups of flour
-2 eggs, beaten and mixed with about a tablespoon of water
-4 cups of frozen french fries
-salt and pepper to taste
-4-5 cups of vegetable oil, for frying
-wooden skewers

"I had to find a way to make kid-friendly meals that are quick and innovative. Obviously, this one goes on the top of the list!"

-Grandma Pam

1. Preheat the oil to about 360 degrees.
2. Meanwhile, season the chicken strips with salt, pepper, and garlic powder.
3. Set up a dredging station by putting the flour in one bowl with a bit of salt and pepper. In a second bowl, add the egg mixture and season it with salt and pepper, as well. In a third bowl, add the frozen French fry crumbs. Make them by putting the frozen French fries into a food processor and pulsing them until the fries turn into crumbs.
4. To prepare the chicken, dip the strips into flour first, then into the egg mixture, then into the French fry crumbs. Then, thread each strip onto a skewer and then deep fry until golden brown.

NOTE: It's a good idea to let the strips rest for a few minutes after you coat them, but before you fry them. This gives the coating enough time to adhere to the chicken strips.

salads, soups, and stews

The Church Ladies and Their Potato Salad

Growing up for anyone can be difficult. Growing up in the context of boundaries and limits, well, that's even more difficult. I was a church kid. There's no other way to put it. Sometimes, I was in church 3 or 4 days a week. Churches don't really do it like they used to anymore. When I was growing up, we had to go to church all day. It was an event. It started with Sunday school. Then, after Sunday school, there'd be breakfast at church. Then after breakfast, there'd be the actual church service. As a kid, I'm not sure why I got so sleepy during this time. It could have been combination of a fulfilling breakfast and having to sit through a few hours of something I don't even think I was that interested in. Then, if you were lucky, there'd be an afternoon service. The afternoon service always started at the same time, 3:30 PM. This was an extended church service whereby the parishioners would take time to celebrate something monumental. I feel like this event happened so often that we celebrated for nearly anything: the pastor's anniversary, the first lady's anniversary, the ushers' anniversary, the deacons' anniversary, or the choir's anniversary. Every week there was a need to celebrate someone's anniversary. How we managed to do that 52 weeks out of the year was amazing, but it happened. What happened between the morning service and the afternoon service was what I lived for.

About three quarters of the way through the morning service when the minister was in high gear, there'd be a scent that released itself in the room. It was unmistakable. The first time you smelled it, you instinctively tricked yourself into believing that what you thought you were smelling wasn't really what you were smelling. But, that doesn't work because it gets stronger and stronger. Suddenly, you're awake and fully alert by the delicious and unmistakable smell of basement fried chicken. We called it 'basement fried chicken' because most church kitchens were in the basement. My local church was no exception. The older ladies would gather to whip up some of the best soul food you would ever experience. This was what would nurture you between the all day church services.

My church cooking ladies were better than anyone else's. Not that I had much experience with the competition, but instinctively, this is what I told myself. It's true because one of the church ladies made this potato salad and at the first bite, you really believed that God was real. It's hard to explain it directly. It was sort of like small diced or mashed potatoes, but mixed with a certain tang and sweetness that really made it over the moon. Tried as I might, I never saw her actually make it. But, every time we celebrated a church occasion, it tasted the exact same - good.

I remember when I was old enough to find out the scoop on it, I'd say, "what do you put in it? It's so good." She'd look at me and say, "Daris!" (because the older church ladies never called me by my 3 syllable name DAR-I-IUS) "It's easy, just cut up your potatoes, then add some of this, and a little of that, and season it real good and that's all to it." Years later, I've never perfected their recipe. But, like most classics, you celebrate them, not replicate them. So, I did. My version is tasty, I promise. But, until you've celebrated a church anniversary, you really haven't had amazing potato salad.

eld: Makes 6 servings | prep time: *5 minutes* | cook time: *15 minutes*

Ingredients

Potato Salad Dressing
2 1/2 cups of good mayo
1/2 cup of sour cream
1/4 cup of Dijon mustard
1 teaspoon of Kosher salt
1 teaspoon of black pepper
1/2 teaspoon of paprika
1/2 teaspoon of garlic powder
1/2 teaspoon of onion powder
1/4 cup of sugar
1 tablespoon of apple cider
vinegar

2 pounds of Russet potatoes,
peeled, diced, boiled & drained
1/2 cup of finely diced onion
1/2 cup of finely diced celery
1/2 cup of finely diced green bell
pepper
3 boiled eggs, chopped
(optional)

"You have to add the dressing while the potatoes are still wam. If you miss this step, don't even bother. Just run down to a deli and pick up a jar of theirs!"

-Grandma Pam

1. In a large bowl, mix all the ingredients for the dressing and keep refrigerated until you're ready to use. (This step can be done ahead)

2. To assemble the salad, after cooking the potatoes, drain them well and toss them back into the hot pan for 2-3 minutes. The heat from the pan will allow the extra moisture to escape the potatoes.

3. Once the potatoes are fully drained, toss them into a large bowl and mix in the onion, celery, and bell pepper. If you're using eggs, this would be a good time to toss them in. Mix well.

4. Add the dressing to the bowl and mix well to combine.

5. Refrigerate the potato salad for at least an hour before enjoying.

NOTE: Be sure to drain the potatoes of all the excess water. Drain them in a strainer first, then throw them back in the hot pot for a few minutes. The heat of the pot will help more of the water escape. It's your 'fully drained potato' insurance policy!

eld: *Makes 8 servings* | prep time: *15 minutes* | cook time: *2 hours*

Ingredients

1 smoked turkey wing or 4 moked turkey tails (if you can nd them)

8 cups of water

2 cups of chicken stock

2 cups of beef stock

4 10oz cans of red kidney eans, rinsed and drained

1 onion, diced

1 green bell pepper, diced

2 ribs of celery, diced

6 garlic cloves, smashed

2 bay leaves

1 tablespoon of dried thyme

1 tablespoon of dried oregano

1 teaspoon of red pepper lakes

1 teaspoon of Cajun easoning

3 tablespoons of olive oil

salt and pepper to taste

4 cups of cooked rice

"**Smoked turkey is easy to find these days. But, if you want make it interesting, add a some thick cut smoked bacon, diced smoked pork chops, or even a ham hock will do!**"

-Grandma Pam

1. Start by boiling the smoked turkey in water for about 30 minutes until the turkey starts to break down a bit.

2. Then, add the beans, onion, bell pepper, celery, garlic, bay leaves, thyme, oregano, red pepper flakes, Cajun seasoning, and olive oil. Stir well to combine and cook on low heat for at least 90 minutes.

3. Be sure to stir the beans to ensure nothing sticks. If the water gets too low, alternately add chicken stock and beef stock so that the beans don't dry out.

4. Once the beans are done, they'll be tender and some will have broken down to resemble a thick sauce or gravy. Taste and adjust the seasoning with salt and pepper, if necessary.

5. Serve by pouring the beans over cooked rice.

NOTE: Some will frown at this, but if done right, canned beans can taste amazing. Plus, they're halfway cooked so they decrease the cooking time by at least half. Just remember to rinse them well. The solution they come packed in is full of a preserving liquid and it doesn't taste good at all.

CHICKEN & WAFFLE *Caesar salad*

yield: *Makes 4 servings* | prep time: *15 minutes* | cook time: *30 minutes*

Ingredients

For the Caesar dressing
-2 cloves of garlic, minced
-1 teaspoon of anchovy paste
-2 tablespoons of fresh lemon juice
-1 teaspoon of Dijon mustard
-1 teaspoon of Worcestershire sauce
-1 cup of mayo
-1/2 cup of grated Parmesan cheese
-1/4 teaspoon of salt
-1/4 teaspoon of ground black pepper

-2 cups of fried chicken nuggets
-6 cups of chopped Romaine lettuce
-4 frozen waffles
-Parmesan cheese shavings

For the waffle croutons
-2 tablespoons of melted butter
-1 teaspoon of dried parsley
-1 teaspoon of garlic powder
-1/2 teaspoon of salt
-1/2 teaspoon of ground black pepper

"Be sure you use a sheet tray to bake the waffle croutons. You want them crunchy on the outside and chewy on the inside! A sheet tray is your crunchy crouton insurance policy!"

-Grandma Pam

1. For the dressing, using a large bowl, whisk all the ingredients together well. Then, refrigerate the dressing until you're ready to use it.

2. For the croutons, preheat the oven to 375 degrees.

3. In a large bowl, combine the melted butter, dried parsley, garlic powder, salt, and black pepper. Then, cut the waffles into bite sized pieces and toss them well in the butter mixture.

4. Arrange the waffles on a sheet tray and bake until they're crispy.

5. To assemble the salad, toss the dressing together with the lettuce, fried chicken nuggets, and waffle croutons. Garnish with Parmesan cheese shavings.

NOTE: Wait until the very last moment before adding the salad dressing to the salad. The best thing about a Caesar salad is the crisp and crunch from the lettuce. Tossing it too early will prevent that from happening.

PEA & CHEDDAR SALAD *with Cajun grilled shrimp*

Ingredients

For the salad dressing

- 1 cup of good mayo
- 1 cup of sour cream
- 1 tablespoon of onion powder
- 2 tablespoons of sugar
- 1/2 tablespoon of garlic powder
- 1 teaspoon of salt
- 1 tablespoon of pepper
- 2 tablespoons of apple cider vinegar

For the salad

- 4 cups of frozen peas, thawed
- 2 cups of cubed cheddar cheese

For the shrimp

- 1 pound of shrimp, cleaned and deveined
- 1 tablespoon of Old Bay seasoning
- 1 teaspoon of Kosher salt
- 2 tablespoons of olive oil

"As soon as the shrimp are just about done, take them out of the oven. The last thing you want with this salad is overcooked shrimp. It's rubbery. It's tasteless. It's no good!"

-Grandma Pam

1. For the salad dressing, combine all the ingredients and whisk together until they're incorporated well and the dressing is smooth. Then, refrigerate until you're ready to use it.

2. To assemble the salad, add the peas and cheese to a large bowl. Add as much of the dressing as desired and mix well. Keep the salad refrigerated until you're ready to serve.

3. To prepare the shrimp, preheat the oven to 400 degrees. Meanwhile, toss the shrimp with the Old Bay seasoning, Kosher salt, and olive oil. Arrange on a sheet tray and roast for about 7 minutes or until the shrimp are just cooked through.

4. To serve the salad, add the salad to a bowl and top with the roasted shrimp.

NOTE: Let the salad base be your play ground. You can add all types of fruits or veggies to the pea salad. And don't stop with shrimp. Any grilled seafood or grilled chicken would totally work great with this recipe!

ENGLISH CUCUMBER *salad with balsamic dressing*

yield: *Makes 6 servings* | prep time: *15 minutes* | cook time: *no cook time needed!*

Ingredients

For the dressing

-1 cup of good olive oil
-1/4 cup of balsamic vinegar
-2 teaspoons of sugar
-1/2 teaspoon of salt
-1/2 teaspoon of pepper
-1 garlic clove minced
-1 tablespoon of Dijon mustard

-2 English cucumbers, sliced

"The best thing about this recipe is that it's healthy, but you wouldn't know it by the taste. Make sure the salad is served cold and you'll become addicted!"

—Grandma Pam

1. To make the dressing, using a large bowl, combine the sugar, salt, pepper, garlic clove, and Dijon mustard until all combined. Then, whisk in the balsamic vinegar.

2. Stream in the olive oil while whisking together the contents in the bowl.

3. Toss in the cucumbers and mix well. Then, refrigerate until you're ready to serve.

NOTE: English cucumbers are best because they don't have a lot of seeds. If you can't find them, regular cucumbers or pickling cucumbers will work, too. Just take a moment to get rid of the seeds in the middle of the cucumber first.

LOW COOKER SHORT RIB *and sweet potato stew*

yield: *Makes 6 servings* | prep time: *5 minutes* | cook time: *about 4 hours*

Ingredients

4 pounds of short ribs
2 large sweet potatoes, cut into cubes
4 cups of beef stock
2 cups of red wine
1 cup of diced onion
4 garlic cloves, chopped
1 bay leaf
1 teaspoon of dried thyme
1 teaspoon of dried oregano
1 teaspoon of salt
1 tablespoon of black pepper
1 tablespoon of cold water
1 tablespoon of cornstarch
cilantro, to garnish

"I know just how pricey short ribs can be. They're not always on sale. With this method of cooking, almost any type of beef would work. If pot roast is on sale, then use pot roast instead of short ribs."

-Grandma Pam

1. Add the short ribs, beef stock, red wine, onion, garlic, bay leaf, thyme, oregano, salt, and pepper to a slow cooker.

2. If you're using a low setting, cook the stew for 8 hours. If you're using a high setting, cook the stew for 4 hours.

3. One (1) hour before the stew is scheduled to be done, mix together the cornstarch and water until the cornstarch has dissolved. Add the cornstarch slurry and diced sweet potatoes to the stew. Cook for an additional 1 hour.

4. Serve the stew by garnishing with cilantro. Enjoy while warm.

NOTE: If you don't have a slow cooker or crock pot, no worries. Instead, throw the ingredients into a Dutch oven or an oven safe dish. Pop the lid on or seal it tightly with aluminum foil and follow the rest of the steps. You'll be fine!

My Aunt Sadie

Our immediate family wasn't that large. Actually, it was very small. There was my grandmother. She was the matriarch. Then, there was my aunt and my mother. My granny divorced my granddaddy a while back. I don't even think I was born yet. Then, for a while it was just my cousin and I. That was our family. It was all we had. I was supposed to have an uncle, but he died before he was born. We had a much larger extended family. My granddaddy had like 8 or 9 siblings. I lose count, but there were a lot. Then, those 8 or 9 had quite a few kids of their own. Now, those few have kids of their own. At this point, I've got so many cousins that I can't keep count. The Williams Crew! As I grew up, we would get together for the holidays. There was a grab bag event during Christmas. There was usually a BBQ at some point during the summer. Although these were technically my Granny's in-laws, you couldn't tell her that. She loved these get-togethers with a passion.

The food was always a highlight. All of the women in my family can cook. I get it completely honest. I don't mean they can just cook a little bit. They can completely throw down and annihilate a kitchen. When they're done setting it out you're sure the heavenly angels are rejoicing. My aunt, Sadie, had a particular culinary anointing. To this day, I don't know a woman who can create such masterpieces without even trying. She bakes cakes and pies. She cooks chickens and beef. She does it all. She is particularly known for her potato salad. I can't begin to describe it.

The flavors meld together like symphonic harmonies. One angle of flavor compliments the other perfectly. The potatoes have been cooked to the right amount of doneness. They're firm, but soft enough to be pillowy. She chooses potatoes with the right amount of starch so that the potatoes serve as a vehicle to carry all the other components. She dices vegetables. I know they're vegetables because they have a certain fresh crunch that's unmistakable. The only thing I don't think I was able to really quite figure out was what type of vegetables. The music my taste buds danced to sounded like crunchy fresh green bell pepper mixed with savory sweet celery and a little zip from some onion. The dance was sweet, tender, subtle, yet efficient. The sauce that encompassed each potato like a freshly snowed-on bush was nothing less than amazing. It was a creamy delight mixture of mayo that was balanced out by the sweetness of a little sugar and the sharp kick of yellow mustard. It wasn't just the ingredients, but it was how she added and incorporated them. She didn't need to taste it to make sure the flavors were on point, she could literally look with her eyes and she'd know just how much of each ingredient she needed to add. My aunt Sadie!

side dishes

Picking Greens: Our Saturday Night Ritual

My cousin is pretty cool. She's always been cool. Growing up, she had cool friends, used to go to cool parties, and just lived an all around cool life. She's four years older than me, so I've always looked up to her. No matter how crazy life got, we bonded. Sometimes, I'd be home when she would get home from school. One of the first things she'd do was turn on the cable box and turn to BET to watch "videos." The BET channel on Prime Cable was 22. I've really always had an old soul. Give me Luther, Patti, or Stevie any day over some of today's current R&B and I'll be happy. See, Luther could sing about a chair in a Section 8 apartment and turn it into a love song. This was the kind of music I gravitated towards. Besides, if your mother and grandmother listened to it while cleaning the house on a Saturday morning, then that's the kind of music I'd probably like.

When I think about it, we always had Sunday dinners. Some were a little lower key than others. But, there was always something good brewing. For the really important dinners, the kind where a few family members would come over, greens were always on the menu. We would eat collards, mustard, and turnips. If you can name the green, we ate it. I don't think I ever knew much about the actual process of cooking greens when I was a kid. But, I knew how to pick them. That was the job of my cousin and I. We were expert green pickers. We'd go in the living room and grab two huge garbage bags. We'd pick the green leaf from the stem very carefully. We'd throw the stem away and then we'd put all of the greens in the other bag. It would take us what seemed like hours to complete this process. We sat on that floor with those big garbage bags in between our legs and we picked leaf after leaf. We did. We'd be watching a television show or a movie on TV until we were all done. This is how we spent many Saturday nights.

Now, I rarely pick greens. I've become quite fond of the stem. It's loaded with nutritional value and it's super flavorful. Besides, I paid for it, so I might as well eat it. I give my greens a rough chop and then I wash them several times until they're super clean. Washing greens is a process. It takes a while, but it's a step you can't miss. Somewhere between sloshing the greens around in warm water and adding them to a pot, I stop and smile. I smile at the memories. Years later, I'm still washing greens the way I saw my grandmother do them. Some things you just don't change.

SPICY BRAISED *collard greens with smoked turkey*

yield: *Makes 8 servings* | prep time: *5 minutes* | cook time: *60 minutes*

Ingredients

-5 bunches of collard greens, rinsed, trimmed, and chopped
-1 pound of smoked turkey tails (smoked turkey wings or drumsticks will work, too)
-3 cups of chicken stock
-3 cups of beef stock
-water, if needed
-5 cloves of garlic
-2 tablespoons of granulated garlic
-1 tablespoon of red pepper flakes
-2 tablespoons of Cajun seasoning
-2 tablespoons of sugar

"This is my go-to recipe for all things collard greens. They're spicy and savory. They're perfect for any Sunday or holiday meal!"

—Grandma Pam

1. Add the beef and chicken stock to a large pot, bring to a boil. Add the collard greens and smoked turkey to the pot. Cook for about 45 minutes or until the greens are tender and the smoked turkey has started to break down.

2. If the stock gets too low, add water.

3. When the greens are tender, add in the garlic cloves, granulated garlic, red pepper flakes, Cajun seasoning, and sugar.

4. Cook for about 15 minutes more, then serve.

NOTE: I always wait and season my greens at the toward the end of the cooking process. Doing it this way prevents the spices from losing their potency!

GRANDMA PAM'S *fried sweet corn*

yield: *Makes 4 servings* | prep time: *5 minutes* | cook time: *20 minutes*

Ingredients

- 5 strips of bacon, cut in pieces
- 1 cup of diced onion
- 4 cloves of minced garlic
- 2 tablespoons of olive oil
- 4 cups of frozen corn
- 1 red bell pepper, diced
- 1 tablespoon of flour
- 1 cup of chicken stock
- cilantro, to garnish

"There's something about the saltiness of the bacon mixed with the savory elements of the garlic and onion that make this recipe work. If you're not going to use real pork bacon, you're going to miss that dimension of the dish."

—Grandma Pam

1. Sauté the bacon in olive oil until the bacon has just about cooked through.
2. Remove the bacon and most of the bacon grease. Then, add the olive oil to the pan and sauté the onion and garlic until fragrant.
3. Then, add in the corn and red bell pepper and cook for about 10 minutes until most of the liquid has cooked out of the pan. You'll need to stir often to ensure nothing sticks.
4. Sprinkle in the flour and cook for about 60 seconds. Then add the chicken stock and cook on low heat until most of the liquid has evaporated and the remaining sauce is super thick.
5. Sprinkle in the bacon and garnish with cilantro to enjoy.

NOTE: There is a lot of starch in corn. It'll make things sticky a bit when cooking this dish. Be sure to stir often to avoid stickage. Yes, stickage!

SPINACH & ARTICHOKE *risotto*

yield: *Makes 6 servings* | prep time: *10 minutes* | cook time: *30 minutes*

Ingredients

- 2 tablespoons of olive oil
- 2 cups of long grain rice
- 4-6 cups of chicken stock
- 2 cups of frozen spinach
- 2 cups of diced artichoke hearts
- 2 cloves of chopped garlic
- 1 cup of good white wine
- 1/2 tablespoon of salt
- 1 tablespoon of pepper
- 1/2 cup of good Parmesan cheese
- 1/2 cup of mascarpone cheese
- 2 tablespoons of butter

"Everyone is so afraid to make risotto. It's the easiest thing to do. Just remember two things: keep stirring and keep the heat on medium. If you scorch the rice, it's over!"

-Grandma Pam

1. In a heavy bottom stock pot, heat the oil and add the rice. Toast the rice until it's light golden brown. Be sure to stir often so nothing burns or sticks.

2. Add the white wine and stir until the wine is almost dissolved.

3. Then, add about a half cup or so of chicken stock at a time. Stir occasionally so nothing sticks or burns. Continue this process until the rice is just about cooked through.

4. About 10 minutes or so before the rice is done, stir in the spinach, artichokes, garlic, salt, and pepper.

5. To finish the rice, stir in the Parmesan and mascarpone cheeses and butter. This will give the risotto a creamy texture. Taste and add salt and pepper, if necessary.

NOTE: This recipe uses spinach and artichokes. But, you can use any flavor combination you love - garlic & herb, broccoli & cheese, even chicken and dried chiles! Don't let your risotto adventures stop with this recipe. Let your imagination run wild.

Church's Chicken...and the Hot Sauce

My grandmother wasn't the type of lady who tried new things. For the life of me, I could never remember her trying exotic foods or too many different cuisines. She liked what she liked and that was it. She wasn't fancy or fussy. If it was good, she ate it. If it was simple, she cooked it. If it was nasty, she'd tell you. But, she'd tell you like only a grandmother could. She'd probably say, "Baby, that could use a little more seasoning." Or, she'd suggestively say, "Why don't you put that cornbread back in the oven for a bit more so it gets nice and brown on top?" Meanwhile, you could catch her on the phone dishing the dirt to one of her church lady friends and she'd be telling the real truth. My grandmother had one of those phones that plugged into the wall. The cord was so long that you literally could walk through the entire house with the phone. I'm not sure cell phones were as popular when she was alive. Even if they were, I think my grandmother would have opted against one. After all, she didn't try new things too often. She liked what she liked and that was it.

One thing she absolutely loved was the fried okra down to the Church's Chicken. We had one in our neighborhood. As a matter of fact, it's still there today. We would stop over for chicken in between church services on Sunday. I would catch her and some of her choir lady friends indulging wearing their Sunday's black and white. They'd have their hairdos done up and they all had pearls around their necks. They'd be eating their chicken, eating their fried okra, and fellowshipping, which I always took for a little church lady gossip. My grandmother used to get the packs of hot sauce and she'd put it all over her chicken and okra. That was one combination that she absolutely loved. To this day, every time I walk past that Church's Chicken, I look in the window and I can see my grandmother and her church lady friends. I see their pearls and their packets of empty hot sauce on the table. They loved their hot sauce.

CRISPY OKRA *with chili-lime salt*

yield: *Makes 4 servings* | prep time: *7 minutes* | cook time: *10 minutes*

Ingredients

- 1 pound of fresh okra
- 4-6 cups of canola oil
- Chili-lime salt (recipe to follow)
- paper towels for draining

Chili-Lime Salt

- 2 tablespoons of Kosher salt
- 1 1/2 teaspoons of sugar
- 1/2 teaspoon of garlic powder
- 1 tablespoon of chili powder
- 1 tablespoon of grated lime zest
- 1/2 teaspoon of black pepper

Just combine each of the ingredients well and store in an air tight container until you're ready to use.

"If you're note an okra fan, try this recipe. It won't end up slimy and this is the only way you'll eat it from now on. Trust me!"

-Grandma Pam

1. In a large skillet or pot, preheat the oil to 365 degrees.
2. Meanwhile, cut each of the okra into length-wise slices.
3. When the oil is ready, drop each of the okra slices into the oil and fry until golden brown & crispy. This should take about 2-3 minutes.
4. Remove the okra from the oil. Place on a paper towel to absorb any excess oil
5. Sprinkle with chili-lime salt while the okra are still hot and enjoy.

NOTE: The key to this recipe is the chili-lime salt. Be sure to sprinkle the okra with the salt as soon as they come out of the oil. This is your chance to really make sure the seasoning sticks to the okra, not the paper towel you're using to drain them.

Her Favorite Midnight Snack

My granny was one funny lady. She wasn't too large in stature, but she wasn't small either. She was hefty and carried it quite well. My grandmother was full of life. She'd give you a mean side eye, she might even talk about you, but she would give you her life if you needed it. It was hard to get her to change her mind once it was made up. Firm. That's what I'd call her. My grandmother was firm. She was that way with everybody else. With me though, I was her soft spot.

She had gone into the hospital for the last time. We had to call the ambulance first. They picked her up and took her to the emergency room. She was really out of it. I don't know if she was sedated or had gone crazy, but she wasn't herself at all. The emergency doctor was as white as they came with strawberry blonde hair and crystal blue eyes. She kept calling him "Darius." She kept saying, "Hey Darius?" or "Darius, stop doing that!" I could hear her. She was talking to me, but directing it to that white doctor.

I sat in the waiting room for a bit before I headed back to her apartment. I lived with her. The hospital was a few blocks away and it was a crisp autumn evening. As I walked, I thought about so much. I remembered that time I was asleep. There's something about sleeping in my grandmother's bed that was soothing. I don't know if it was the pink heavy comforter. Or, perhaps it was the faint smell of some Avon beauty product imbedded in the fabric. Whatever it was, it was amazing. This one time, it was a hot Chicago summer evening, so the box fan was going. That was our air conditioner back then. You'd open the windows, put a box fan in every window, and turn off the lights. This was supposed to cool down the house. If you formed your mind just right, you sort of believed that it worked. You would pay no attention to the sweat dripping down your back; you would believe you were cool.

It was the middle of the night and I turned over because I heard a noise. I heard footsteps moving about, one drag of a house shoe at a time. The house shoe drags were becoming louder and louder. Suddenly, they stopped. Then, I heard this crinkly sound. Then came this crunch crunch crunch and the crinkly sound again. Then, the footsteps started and then faded away, one drag of a house shoe at a time. As I drifted back off to sleep, I thought to myself that she just wanted a little taste of her favorite dill flavored potato chips for a little midnight snack.

ROASTED POTATOES *with dill chimichurri*

yield: *Makes 4 servings* | prep time: *10 minutes* | cook time: 18-20 *minutes*

Ingredients

-3 pounds of your favorite potato, cut into 2 inch discs
-1 1/2 tablespoons of Kosher salt
-1 tablespoon of black pepper
-1/4 cup of good olive oil
-dill chimichurri, recipe to follow

Dill Chimichurri
-1 cup of fresh dill sprigs, chopped finely
-2 cloves of minced garlic
-2 tablespoons of apple cider vinegar
-2 tablespoons of sugar
-1/4 cup of good olive oil
-a pinch of red pepper flakes

For the chimichurri, just combine all ingredients in a large bowl and refrigerate for at least an hour before eating.

"Throw a little salt in the water when you boil the potatoes. Whatever's in the water will get absorbed into the potatoes. No flavor in the water? No flavor in the potatoes!"

-Grandma Pam

1. In a large pot, boil the potatoes for about 6-8 minutes until they've softened, but not completely fork tender. Drain and cool.
2. Preheat the oven to 400 degrees. Meanwhile, using a fork, smash each potato a little so that each disc has it's own personality.
3. Coat evenly with olive oil and season by sprinkling salt and pepper on each smashed disc.
4. Roast in the oven for about 12 minutes or until the potatoes are crispy on the outside.
5. While the potatoes are still warm, top each potato with a bit of dill chimichurri.

NOTE: When boiling potatoes, after you drain them, put them back in the pot. The heat from the pot will allow the water to evaporate even more from the potatoes. Also, be sure to add the chimichurri on while the potatoes are still warm. They'll absorb the sauce much better.

COCONUT YAM RICE *with Jerk fried chicken*

yield: *Makes 6 servings* | prep time: *2 minutes* | cook time: *20 minutes*

Ingredients

- 2 cups of long grain rice
- 2 tablespoons of olive oil
- 1 1/2 cups of chicken stock
- 1 cup of coconut milk
- 1 cup of diced sweet potato
- cilantro, to garnish

"Coconut milk and chicken stock are what make this rice tastes so insanely delicious. It's savory with a hint of sweetness!"

—Grandma Pam

1. In a large skillet, heat the olive oil over medium high heat until it's almost smoking. Then, add the rice and cook for 2-3 minutes. Stir the rice often so nothing sticks or burns.
2. While the rice is toasting, add the diced sweet potato to the skillet.
3. When the rice is light brown and just slightly toasted, add the chicken stock and coconut milk. Reduce the heat to medium low and cook until all the liquid has been absorbed by the rice.
4. Then, turn off the heat, add a lid to the skillet and let the rice sit for at ~~let~~ ᴬᴸᴱᴬˢᵀ 10 minutes.
5. After at least 10 minutes, fluff the rice with a fork and enjoy.

NOTE: The key to rice is simple. First, make sure you toast it. Secondly, be sure to let it stand for about 10 minutes with the lid on. This allows the rice to continue cooking through so that each grain is perfectly tender.

My Aunt Cheryl's Green Beans & White Potatoes

It was more like an unspoken rule. Our immediate family was small. There were only a handful of us. There was my cousin, my mother, my aunt, my grandmother, and I. That's all there was for a while. Eventually, three more made it into the fold and then, my grandmother died. All in all, we are a small bunch in numbers. I don't really remember too many circumstances as to why things happened they way they did. I remember the effects they had on us, both good and bad. The address was 1349 N. Kostner in Chicago. That's deep in the West Side. All of us lived in a small 2-bedroom apartment. There was a living room, a kitchen, a bathroom, and two bedrooms.

My aunt and mother did as best as they could to carry the traditions of my grandmother. I remember still going to church almost every Sunday. We would get there late, but we were there. I would see my grandmother there. She sang in the choir. She was always on the front row. We would make eye contact and she'd smile at me to let me know she saw me. Just like it was with my grandmother, Sunday dinners were still a big deal. I remember us all going grocery shopping together. Back then we were poor. I didn't realize just how poor we were. As a kid, you don't have a concept of these types of things. We lived on a weekday diet of Spam and Ramen noodles. But, that was a great combo and it tasted good. So you never knew you were poor because you ate food that tasted good.

My aunt didn't have many recipes in her repertoire. It wasn't that she was a bad cook, I guess she only knew how to cook a few things. The dishes that she did cook were amazing. One of them was her recipe for boiled green beans and white potatoes. My cousin and I would be in charge of snapping the green beans. We'd work in harmony to snap the ends off the green beans, and then we'd snap them in half. We'd throw them in a bag so that they could get washed well and then added to a pot that had been boiling for an hour with a few ham hocks. My aunt would season the green beans and then add in white potatoes. I'm sure those green beans were cooked until they had no more nutritional value. However, they were the juiciest and most savory green beans you'd ever eat.

SAUTÉED GREEN BEANS *with crispy potatoes*

yield: *Makes 4 servings* | prep time: *10 minutes* | cook time: *20 minutes*

Ingredients

-1 pound of fresh green beans, with the stem removed
-2 cloves of garlic, sliced
-1 pound of potatoes, cut into 2 inch pieces
-3 tablespoons of olive oil, divided
-1 tablespoon of Kosher salt, divided
-1 tablespoon of pepper, divided
-1 pinch of red pepper flakes
-2 tablespoons of butter

"Any potato will work. But, be sure to use parchment paper. The starch in the potatoes will make them stick to the pan. You want to spend your time eating, not scraping."

—Grandma Pam

1. Preheat the oven to 400 degrees.

2. In a large bowl, toss the potatoes with 1/2 tablespoon of salt, 1/2 tablespoon of pepper, 2 tablespoons of olive oil

3. Arrange on a sheet tray and roast until fork tender and crispy.

4. Sauté the fresh green beans and garlic in the remaining olive oil and butter until the green beans area tender. Then, season with the remaining salt and pepper and red pepper flakes.

5. Toss the roasted potatoes with the green beans and serve warm or room temperature.

NOTE: The best vessel to roast in is a sheet tray. It has low sides which allows for the heat to attack the potatoes at all sides while they're roasting. This is your crispy potato insurance policy!

CHILI GARLIC CABBAGE

yield: Makes 6 servings | prep time: 4 minutes | cook time: 15 minutes

Ingredients

- 1 head of cabbage, cut into sliced
- 2 3 tablespoons of olive oil
- 1 teaspoon of red pepper flakes
- 1 1/2 teaspoons of kosher salt
- 1 teaspoon of black pepper
- 1 1/2 tablespoons of apple cider vinegar
- 6 cloves of garlic, sliced
- 2 tablespoons of sugar

"There is no excuse. Be sure to wash the cabbage thoroughly after you clean it. Then, drain it well. You don't want the excess liquid cooking in the pan."

—Grandma Pam

1. In a large skillet, heat the oil and add the sliced garlic. Cook for just a few minutes over medium heat until the garlic is fragrant and barely toasted.
2. Quickly add the cabbage to the pan in batches so that the pan cools down a bit and the cabbage cooks evenly. Stir often to make sure each cabbage leaf is coated in garlic oil.
3. When the cabbage has wilted and reduced considerably, add the salt, pepper, apple cider vinegar, and sugar.
4. After adding the seasonings, cook the cabbage for 3-4 more minutes. Stir well to ensure the seasoning is well distributed throughout the cabbage.

NOTE: For this dish, you can substitute olive oil for coconut oil, garlic flavored oil, or even bacon fat. Be sure you're using a large enough skillet to work with. Also, don't fret. When you add all of the cabbage at first, it looks like it's a lot. And it is. However, the cabbage will eventually cook down.

GRILLED CORN ON THE COB with honey butter

Yield: Makes 4 servings | prep time: 8 minutes | cook time: 15 minutes

Ingredients

- 4 ears of fresh corn
- 2 tablespoons of olive oil
- 4 tablespoons of butter
- 4 tablespoons of honey
- 1 teaspoon of Kosher salt

"Fresh is always best. If fresh corn isn't in season, skip this recipe! Do yourself a favor and don't try this with frozen corn on the cob. It just won't work."

—Grandma Pam

1. Preheat a grill pan until it's super hot.

2. Meanwhile, coat each ear of corn well with the olive oil. Then, grill in a grill pan on all sides.

3. In a separate sauce pan, melt the butter and honey and then drizzle it over the grilled corn.

4. Finish by sprinkling each ear of corn with a bit of Kosher salt.

NOTE: This recipe works great using an indoor grill pan on the stove. However, using a charcoal grill outside takes this recipe to a whole other level. The smokiness from the grill mixed with the sweet corn is a perfect balance of flavors.

SPINACH & ARTICHOKE *twice baked potatoes*

yield: *Makes 4 servings* | prep time: *15 minutes* | cook time: *30 minutes*

Ingredients

- 4 large Russet potatoes
- 1 cup of mascarpone cheese
- 2 cloves of minced garlic
- 1 tablespoon of salt
- 1 tablespoon of pepper
- 1/2 cup of white cheddar cheese
- 1 1/2 cups of frozen spinach, drained
- 3/4 cup of diced artichoke hearts
- olive oil

"Do what I do. Bake up a few potatoes ahead of time. Keep some in the fridge. When you're ready to enjoy this recipe, start at step #2. You're already ahead of the game!"

-Grandma Pam

1. On a large baking sheet, roast the potatoes until they're fork tender. Then, set them aside to cool.
2. Once the potatoes have cooled to the touch, slice them in half lengthwise and scoop out the inside. Be sure to leave about a half inch border around the inside of the potato.
3. In a large bowl, mix together the potato, mascarpone cheese, garlic, salt, pepper, white cheddar cheese, spinach and artichokes. Then pile the filling back inside the potato skins.
4. Bake the potatoes until they've heated through and have gotten slightly golden brown on top. Drizzle with olive oil and serve.

NOTE: Russet potatoes work best because they're big hearty potatoes. But, don't let that stop you. Just about any variety of potato will work with this recipe - even sweet potatoes!

yield: *Makes 6 servings* | prep time: *5 minutes* | cook time: *45 minutes*

Ingredients

- 2 pounds of Russet potatoes, cut into discs
- 2 cups of half and half
- 1 tablespoon of cornstarch
- 4 cloves of garlic, sliced
- 3/4 tablespoon of salt
- 1 tablespoon of pepper
- 1/2 teaspoon of nutmeg
- 2 cups of shredded white cheddar cheese
- 1 tablespoon of dried Italian herbs

"This recipe is so easy and it tastes so good. If you get caught up into your favorite soap opera and leave it in the oven too long, it doesn't matter. The cheese gets cooked more into the potatoes and it's even tastier that way!"

—Grandma Pam

1. Preheat the oven to 350 degrees. In a large bowl, mix the half and half with the cornstarch. Then whisk in the salt, pepper, dried Italian herbs and nutmeg.

2. Arrange the potatoes in a baking dish and tuck the sliced garlic cloves all throughout the potatoes.

3. Sprinkle the cheddar cheese over the potatoes in an even layer. Then carefully pour over the half and half mixture.

4. Bake the whole dish for 30-35 minutes or until the sauce has thickened and the potatoes have cooked through. Serve while the potatoes are still hot.

NOTE: Try combining various types of cheeses to make this dish. In particular, anything that's got a creamy texture will work. Try it with Swiss, Fontina, or even Gouda!

SMOKED GOUDA *corn pudding*

Ingredients

- 2 tablespoons of butter
- 1 tablespoon of flour
- 2 cups of half and half
- 1/2 teaspoon of nutmeg
- 1 teaspoon of salt
- 1 teaspoon of pepper
- 1/2 teaspoon of garlic powder
- 2 cups of shredded smoked gouda
- 4 cups of corn kernels (fresh or frozen)

"The best advice I can give you is be sure you cook the flour and butter together long enough. If you don't the sauce ends up tasting pasty. That's great for arts and crafts…not so much for corn pudding!"
—*Grandma Pam*

1. Preheat the oven to 350 degrees. Meanwhile, melt the butter in a large pot and sprinkle in the flour. While stirring, cook the butter and flour together for about 90 seconds. Then, whisk in the half and half.
2. Bring the mixture to a boil. Then reduce the heat. Season the sauce with nutmeg, salt, pepper, and garlic powder. Stir in 1 1/2 cups of the smoked gouda and all of the corn kernels.
3. Pour the mixture into an oven safe dish and top with the remaining cheese.
4. Bake in the oven until golden brown. This should take about 13-15 minutes. Enjoy while it's still warm.

NOTE: Smoked gouda and corn are like a match made in heaven. That's true of most cheeses. So, with that being said, if you can't find smoked gouda, don't worry. Any good melting cheese will work. If you've got a good cheddar, it'll be just as tasty!

WINTER SUCCOTASH *with bacon*

ield: *Makes 6 servings* | prep time: *5 minutes* | cook time: *25 minutes*

Ingredients

- 2 cups of frozen lima beans
- 1 cup of frozen corn
- 1 cup of frozen black eyed peas
- 1/2 cup of diced bell pepper
- 1/2 cup of diced onion
- 2 cloves of garlic, chopped
- 5 strips of bacon, cut into pieces
- 1/2 cup of good white wine
- 2 tablespoons of olive oil
- 1 teaspoon of Kosher salt
- 1 teaspoon of black pepper
- 1/2 teaspoon of dried thyme

"**Adding bacon to anything makes it taste good. This dish can be made any time of year. Of course, fresh is always best. However, if you've got a hankering for this recipe and you can't get access to fresh, frozen will work just fine!"**

—Grandma Pam

1. In a skillet, sauté the bacon, onion and garlic together in olive oil until the bacon has just cooked through. Then, add in the lima beans, corn, black eyed peas, and bell pepper. Season the vegetables with salt and pepper.

2. Cook the succotash until the lima beans are a bit tender. This should take about 15 minutes on medium heat. Then, add the white wine and dried thyme.

3. Cook the succotash until the white wine has completely reduced. Taste the dish and if necessary, adjust seasonings by adding more salt or pepper. Serve while warm.

NOTE: Traditionally, the rule of thumb for succotash is to add lima beans. However, rules were made to be broken. Toss in any type of bean that you love. The seasonings, especially the white wine, in this recipe will work just fine.

I'm Black. Collards are to me what platanos are to Latinos. It's what green tea is to the Chinese. It's the gefilte fish to Jews. It's the borsch to Russians. It's my Sunday after church healing. Collards mixed with corn bread are what allow breath to enter my body. Collards affirm the resurrection. Collards are indeed the anointing that reclaims what's been lost. It's just what we ate. It's what I know.

Traditionally, collards were thought of as a poor man's vegetable. They take a long time to cook. They're particularly tough and not enjoyable if they're not done right. Because of this, they're cheap. In many cases, this was all my family was able to afford. So, we ate them. A lot! Because they were made with love and tasted amazing, I was none the wiser.

I try to work collards in as many ways as I can. Today, it's with pesto. The concept is easy. You mix blanched collards with garlic, pecans, and olive oil. But when you think about the endless possibilities,

COLLARD GREEN PESTO *roasted tomatoes*

yield: *Makes 4 servings* | prep time: *10 minutes* | cook time: *16 minutes*

Ingredients

-2 pints of cherry tomatoes
-1 cup of collard green pesto, recipe to follow

For the collard green pesto
-3 cups of collard green leaves (if using frozen, be sure to thaw and drain well)
-1/2 cup of toasted pecans
-1/2 cup of grated Parmesan cheese
-1 teaspoon of salt
-1 teaspoon of pepper
-3 garlic cloves
-1 1/2 cups of olive oil

"**If you notice, you can use frozen collard greens for this recipe. While, I'd never use frozen collards for a Sunday meal, I'd totally use them for this pesto. It saves time and tastes just as great!**
-Grandma Pam

1. Preheat the oven to 350 degrees. Meanwhile, to make the pesto, just throw all of the ingredients except for the olive oil in to a blender or food processor. Start the blade, then drizzle in the olive oil slowly. Make sure the olive oil is combined well with the rest of the ingredients, then remove and place in a container.

2. To roast the tomatoes, toss them in a large bowl and mix with the pesto.

3. Arrange the tomatoes in a baking dish and roast the tomatoes for 13-16 minutes or until they've bursted a bit and started to turn a little brown.

4. Remove the tomatoes from the pan and if not serving immediately, store them in an air tight container in the refrigerator until you're ready to use them.

NOTE: Not sure what to do with collard green pesto roasted tomatoes? Well, you could eat them as is. They'd make a perfect side dish. Or, you could toss them with pasta, grilled shrimp or chicken, and a sprinkle of Parmesan cheese. Yum!

BALSAMIC & HONEY *roasted Brussels sprouts*

yield: *Makes 3 servings* | prep time: 5 *minutes* | cook time: 15 *minutes*

Ingredients

3 cups of Brussels sprouts, cut in half
-1/2 tablespoon of salt
-1 tablespoon of black pepper
-1 tablespoon of minced garlic
-1/2 cup of balsamic vinegar
-1/3 cup of honey
-2 tablespoons of olive oil

"**The honey is great in this dish. It helps balance the bitterness that Brussels sprouts can sometimes have. Be sure you line your baking dish is parchment paper. It makes clean up time a cinch!"**

-Grandma Pam

1. Preheat the oven to 375 degrees.
2. In a large bowl, mix together the the honey and balsamic vinegar until the honey has been loosened and is well incorporated. Then, toss in the salt, pepper, minced garlic, and olive oil. Mix well to combine.
3. Toss in the Brussels sprouts and mix well. Then, arrange on a sheet tray and roast for 15 minutes or until the sprouts are tender.
4. Serve warm or at room temperature.

NOTE: If you're afraid to try Brussels sprouts, then this is the recipe for you. When cooked, the balsamic and honey do a great job of balancing out the bitterness and offering a really sweet flavor to the Brussels sprouts.

Oprah: My Other Parent

Oprah was huge in our house growing up. I think she was huge in everyone's house. In fact, she was so huge that I never really even thought of Oprah as a real person. I thought she was a thing. Isn't that what 8 year olds do? Sure, I saw her physically on the TV, but my mind couldn't comprehend Oprah the person from Oprah the thing. So, to me, she was huge enough to forego the person status and instead, she was a thing.

What Oprah said, went. Period. I can remember countless conversations between my grandmother and one of her church lady friends. Granny would ask them if they'd seen what had happen on Oprah. For the next 25 minutes, I'd hear them ramble on about the show's topic that day. It felt like everyday Oprah had something new happening. I don't think my grandmother could wait to add it to her repertoire. Whether it was a new way of thinking or a new product or even a new story, my grandmother was all in. I spent a lot more time with my grandmother than I did my mother. But, in many cases, that meant nothing. For my mother, it was Oprah all the way too.

We lived on the west side of Chicago right off Chicago Ave. & Menard St. We were on the 2nd floor. I'll never forget. We lived across the street from an ice cream parlor and on the other side of the street was a local chicken shack. This was really a time when life was good for me. My cousin lived with us at the time. She really was (and still is today) more like a sister than a cousin. We were all we had growing up, so we really had to make it work. I remember nights listening to the local radio station on her pink radio with the antenna pointed out the window. You had to point it out of the window so that you were able to get good reception. If you didn't, you would hear fuzz all night. The window would be open and the nice warm summer breeze knew just where to find me. The words of Michele's "Something in My Heart" would catch a rhythm and somewhere between the commercial break and the start of the next song, I'd fall asleep.

This day, my mother caught a new recipe on the Oprah Show. It was a pretty simple dish, by all standards. The base was plain old white rice. We always bought the rice in the blue and white box. Then, there was a ground beef mixture on top of the rice. The ground beef was topped with broccoli and then stewed tomatoes. It was interesting. It was different. Surprisingly, I liked it. I remember the look my mother had. She had explored new territories and it worked. It eventually became one of our favorite dishes.

STEWED GREENS *and tomatoes*

yield: *Makes 4 servings* | prep time: *10 minutes* | cook time: *1 hour and 15 minutes*

Ingredients

- 4 bunches of fresh collard greens, cleaned and chopped
- 1 onion, diced
- 4 cloves of garlic, minced
- 4 cups of chicken stock
- 2 cups of water
- 1 smoked turkey wing
- 1 tablespoon of Cajun seasoning
- 1 heaping tablespoon of sugar
- 4 tomatoes, sliced

"This is a great alternative to a pot of regular Sunday greens. With this recipe, all you need is a side salad and a glass of ice cold water and you've got yourself a complete meal!"

—Grandma Pam

1. In a large pot, bring the water and chicken stock to a boil, then reduce the heat and add in the turkey wing. Cover the pot and let the turkey wing cook for about 15 minutes.
2. Then, add in the collard greens, onion, and garlic. Cook for about 45 minutes or until the collard greens are tender.
3. Then, add in the Cajun seasoning, sugar, and tomatoes. Stir to combine and let cook for another 15 minutes.
4. Enjoy while warm.

NOTE: If you need a quicker option, frozen greens work best for this recipe too. Don't use the canned stuff. They're full of preservatives that will completely change the flavor profile of the dish.

The Perfect Macaroni & Cheese

Macaroni and cheese is sacred. It's the Ark of the Covenant for many a family meal experience. It's the epicenter of what joins friends and foe. It's the midnight moon that rolls in the tide. It really is one of those things that must be present on any family meal table. Just as with most other recipes, there's an art to getting it right. It's so revered that only a handful of people dare attempt to make it and then serve it to the masses. Literally, every 'I' must be dotted if you're going to attempt to stake claim as the one who made the mac and cheese.

In my family, this, amongst other things, undoubtedly went to my grandmother. I would witness her in the kitchen hours before a meal was to be served. This was a big deal. She stuck to what she knew, too. Now that I look back and remember what she did, it was always the same. She didn't switch it up much because it worked. It just did. She would always use pet milk. I never quite understood that when I was younger. Now that I know better, it's nothing more than a can of evaporated milk. It's got more of a milkier taste and less moisture than regular milk. She used eggs. She always used eggs. I hate eggs. But, she used them. She would always use that box grater to grate the cheddar cheese. And now that I'm writing this, it was cheddar and only cheddar. She rarely deviated. She bought the block cheese because it was on sale. This is a habit I picked up from her and I still practice to this day. She would use that same big white bowl to mix the creamy concoction before putting it in the oven. That bowl served so many purposes. It was the macaroni bowl. It was the bowl to drain the fried fish once it was lined with paper towels. If a cake was being made, it was the mixing bowl for that too. That white bowl wasn't perfect either. It had seen its share of ups and downs. It was faithful. It has burn marks on it because somebody left it too close to something that was cooking in the stove. The side of it had melted a bit. I suppose a hot spoon got a hold of it. But, that's what we used.

The perfect mac and cheese has to be creamy. The sauce needs to be as thick and luscious as the clouds in a summer sun's sky. The pasta can't be overcooked at all. It has to be seasoned just right. Before you even attempt to bake the mac and cheese, everything about the mixture must be perfect. Once you're sure you've got the right amount of cheese, seasonings, and pasta, then you pour the mixture into a baking dish. You mustn't break the cardinal rule of topping the dish with more cheese so that it melts while it bakes. As it bakes, you can smell it. If you give it a few minutes and peek inside, you should see the mac and cheese bubbling and the top browning. That's how you know you've done it right. After it looks perfect, you take the mac and cheese out of the oven and marvel at how pretty it looks. Then, you do what my grandmother did. You grab a fork and sneak a corner piece of the casserole. You've got to make sure it tastes just right.

THE ULTIMATE BAKED *mac and cheese*

yield: *Makes 6 servings* | prep time: *10 minutes* | cook time: *45 minutes*

Ingredients

-4 cups of cooked pasta
-4 tablespoons of butter
-2 tablespoons of flour
-2 cups of half and half
-1 teaspoon of salt
-1 teaspoon of pepper
-1 pinch of garlic powder
-1 pinch of paprika
-1 cup of sour cream
-3 cups of shredded cheese (your choice, but typically Gouda, Cheddar, Fontina and an American cheese product works best)
-shredded cheese, for topping

"The key is the cheese sauce. Taste it as you go along to make sure it's perfect! Also, follow my two simple tips. When boiling the pasta, over salt the water and undercook the pasta!"
-Grandma Pam

1. Preheat the oven to 350 degrees. In a large pot, melt 4 tablespoons of butter. Then, stir in the flour and cook for about 60 seconds while constantly stirring.

2. Whisk in the half and half and continue to stir periodically while on high heat. When the sauce comes to a boil, it will start to thicken.

3. Fold in the cheese, salt, pepper, garlic powder, paprika, and sour cream. Allow the cheese to melt dow into a smooth sauce. This should take about 3-4 minutes on low heat.

4. When the sauce is smooth, mix in the cooked pasta and pour into a baking dish. Top with the shredded cheese and bake until golden brown and bubbly.

NOTE: The list of cheeses that you can add to this dish are endless. Play around with some of your favorites. Use cheddar as a base, but add hard cheeses, creamy cheese, or even stinky cheeses. They'll all work really great with this recipe!

WHIPPED *sweet potatoes with salt*

yield: *Makes 4 servings* | prep time: *5 minutes* | cook time: *30 minutes*

Ingredients

- 3 medium sized sweet potatoes
- 1 stick of butter, room temperature
- 1/3 cup of heavy cream
- 1/2 cup of sugar
- 1 teaspoon of Kosher salt

"If you're like me, you've been candying sweet potatoes for years. Not anymore! One taste of this recipe and this will be your go to recipe for all things sweet potatoes."
—Grandma Pam

1. Preheat the oven to 350 degrees.
2. Wrap each potato in aluminum foil tightly and roast for 25 minutes or until the potatoes are fork tender.
3. After the potatoes have cooled, remove the skins from the potatoes and put the peeled potatoes into a pot or bowl. Heat the butter, sugar, and heavy cream in a pot and then add the hot liquid to the potatoes.
4. Serve the potatoes with a sprinkle of Kosher salt on top.

NOTE: They key to this recipe is really wrapping the potatoes tightly in foil and then letting them bake in the oven. This will develop their sweetness and they'll taste amazing. Be sure to set an oven safe dish under the potatoes as they bake so nothing leaks in the oven.

CREAMED FIELD GREENS *with French fried onions*

Yield: *Makes 4 servings* | prep time: 5 *minutes* | cook time: 15 *minutes*

Ingredients

- 8 cups of your favorite frozen cooking greens, thawed & drained
- 4 tablespoons of butter
- 2 tablespoons of flour
- 3 cloves of garlic, sliced
- 1/2 cup of onion, minced
- 2 cups of heavy cream
- 1 cup of grated Parmesan
- 1 teaspoon of salt
- 1 tablespoon of pepper
- 2 cups of French fried onions

"This is the perfect way to repurpose leftover cooked greens. Sometimes, you might only have a little bit of this or a little bit of that left. Mix them together and turn those leftover greens into an amazing recipe!"

—Grandma Pam

1. In a large skillet, melt the butter over medium heat and add the garlic and onion. Cook the garlic and onion in the butter for about 2 minutes. Then, sprinkle in the flour and cook for another 90 seconds while stirring often.
2. Whisk in the heavy cream and season the sauce with salt and pepper. When the sauce comes to a boil, it will start to thicken. Reduce the heat and add in the greens and Parmesan cheese. Cook for 7-10 minutes on low heat.
3. To serve, top with French fried onions and enjoy while the dish is still hot.

> **NOTE:** As with most recipes in this book, you're totally encouraged to play around with your cheeses. Any hard cheese will work. Instead of Parmesan, try Pecorino, Romano, or even Asiago!

ROASTED VEGGIE *rice pilaf*

Ingredients

- 1/2 cup of diced onion
- 1/2 cup of diced bell pepper
- 1/2 cup of diced celery
- 1/2 cup of diced carrot
- 3 garlic cloves, chopped
- 1 tablespoon of salt
- 1 teaspoon of black pepper
- 2 tablespoons of olive oil

For the rice
- 2 cups of long grain rice
- 2 tablespoons of olive oil
- 4 cups of chicken stock
- cilantro, for garnishing

"The key to perfect rice is simple. Toast it first and then cook it in chicken stock. Whatever is in the liquid gets absorbed in the rice. No flavor in the liquid? No flavor in the rice!"

—Grandma Pam

1. Preheat the oven to 350 degrees. In a bowl, toss the onion, bell pepper, celery, and carrot with the garlic, salt, pepper, and olive oil. Toss to coat well, then arrange on a sheet tray and roast in the oven for 20 minutes or until the vegetables are tender.

2. Meanwhile, to make the rice, sauté the rice in olive oil until it's lightly golden brown.

3. Then stir in the chicken stock. Once all of the stock has cooked out, turn off the heat and put a lid on the pot. Let the rice stand for at least 15 minutes, then fluff with a fork.

4. Toss the roasted vegetables with the rice and garnish with cilantro. Enjoy while the rice is hot.

NOTE: This is a great time to clean out the veggie drawer in your refrigerator. Use whatever veggies you have on hand, especially some that might be turning bad. They'll all work perfectly for this recipe.

OUTHERN STYLE *sausage & cornbread dressing*

eld: *Makes 6 servings* | prep time: *10 minutes* | cook time: *30 minutes*

Ingredients

- 6 cups of crumbled cornbread
- 1 pound of Italian sausage
- 1 cup of diced onion
- 1 cup of diced celery
- 2 garlic cloves, minced
- 1/2 tablespoon of salt
- 1 teaspoon of pepper
- 1 teaspoon of poultry seasoning
- 2 cans of cream of chicken soup
- About 5-6 cups of good chicken stock
- 2 tablespoons of olive oil

"This is my go-to recipe for all things holiday dressing (or stuffing). In fact, this recipe is so easy to whip up, it's a great weeknight side dish that can be thrown together in a short time."

Grandma Pam

1. Preheat the oven to 350 degrees. Meanwhile, sauté the sausage, onion, celery, and garlic together in olive oil until the sausage is just cooked through.
2. Combine the sausage mixture with the cornbread and season with salt, pepper, and poultry seasoning.
3. Add in the cream of chicken soup and stir well to combine.
4. Then, add in the chicken stock about a cup at a time until the desired creamy consistency is reached.
5. Pour the mixture into a baking dish and bake for 30 minutes, uncovered. Then, serve immediately.

NOTE: If you're going for strictly vegetarian on this dish, here are a few tips. Omit the sausage. Nix the cream of chicken soup and chicken stock, too. Instead, use cream of celery or cream of mushroom soup and good veggie stock will do the trick.

main dishes, meats, and seafood

The Big Black Roasting Pan with the White Dots

I was maybe 5 or 6. That was an early enough age to learn many lessons. My childhood household had plenty of lessons to learn. I merely observed and if you can imagine how a 6 year old observes, images were just etched in my memory. Sure, I'll agree that at that age, one isn't able to clearly explain what he's learning. That doesn't mean he's not learning.

Here are a few lessons I've learned from observing. I learned that when you mop the floor, you must wear high heel shoes. I'm assuming this was so that you didn't track the floor as you continued to mop. My grandmother always did this. I'm not sure why. I also learned that you must always add bleach to your dishwater, no matter how many holes developed in the towels. You should always keep the towels for as long as possible. My grandmother would keep dishtowels around for years. I learned that the bacon grease never gets discarded. You must always carefully add it to the coffee can sitting on top of the stove. I also learned that a real Sunday dinner must involve one of the huge black roasting pans with the dome lid. You know, the one that had the little white dots all over it.

I'm not sure why it was as important as it was. One thing I did know is that it was in every Black person's home. Even when we got invited over to someone else's house for a big dinner, out of nowhere, that same gigantic roasting pan would show up. My grandmother would use that pan when she was to do her good cooking. The roasting pan wouldn't come out during regular weeknight dinners. But for Sunday and holiday dinners, it was a must. Whatever was in it, it made my grandmother proud. When she would present its offerings to us, she did so with her chest out and her head held high. She worked to get the dish just right and there would be no other way to serve it than in the huge roasting pan with the dome lid with the white dots.

PEACH BALSAMIC *glazed wings*

yield: *Makes 4 servings* | prep time: *5 minutes* | cook time: *45 minutes*

Ingredients

Peach Balsamic Glaze
-1/2 cup of peach nectar
-1/2 cup of balsamic vinegar
-2 tablespoons of brown sugar
-1 clove of garlic, grated
-1 tablespoon of olive oil
-1 pinch of Kosher salt
-1 teaspoon of black pepper

-2 pounds of chicken wings (about 7-8 wings)
-2 ripe peaches, sliced

*You'll also need something to glaze the chicken with. A pastry brush is your best tool. If you don't have one, you can use a spoon. Just make sure you glaze the entire surface of the chicken.

"If you don't use parchment paper, your chicken will stick. No one likes sticking chicken. You want the chicken on your plate, not stuck in the pan. "

—Grandma Pam

1. Preheat the oven to 375 degrees.

2. In a sauce pot, add the peach nectar, balsamic vinegar, brown sugar, garlic, olive oil, salt, and pepper and cook on medium heat until the mixture comes to a boil. Then, reduce the heat to just above a simmer and cook until the glaze is slightly thickened.

3. Meanwhile, arrange the chicken wings on a sheet tray lined with parchment paper. Then, place in the oven so they start cooking.

4. About 15 minutes into the cooking process, use a pastry brush and brush the chicken with the glaze. Put it back in the oven. Do this every 5-7 minutes until the chicken has cooked completely through. Then remove from the oven and set aside

5. Meanwhile, heat an indoor grill pan on the stove until it's super hot. Grill the peach slices until they're warmed through. Serve the grilled peaches with the delicious glazed chicken.

NOTE: Be sure to glaze the chicken ever 5-7 minutes. This ensures the coating sticks and the chicken is super flavorful once it's done cooking. Also, they key is reducing the glaze to the right thickness. Until you perfect the recipe, start on a low flame. The glaze can go from thick to luscious to burnt and bitter in a matter of seconds.

SRIRACHA GLAZED *chicken wings*

yield: *Makes 6 servings* | prep time: *10 minutes* | cook time: *25 minutes*

Ingredients

-2 pounds of chicken wings, cleaned and patted dry with paper towels
-1 tablespoon of good olive oil
-1 teaspoon of Kosher salt
-1 teaspoon of ground black pepper
-1 teaspoon of garlic powder
-1 cup of Sriracha glaze (recipe to follow)

Sriracha Glaze

-1 1/2 cups of Sriracha hot sauce
-1/2 cup of brown sugar
-1/2 cup of honey
-1/2 tablespoon of salt
-1 teaspoon of black pepper
-1 stick of butter
-2 garlic cloves, minced

"Parchment paper is your friend with this recipe. Use it so nothing, especially this sticky glaze, sticks to the pan."
—Grandma Pam

1. To make the glaze, combine the sriracha, brown sugar, honey, salt, black pepper, butter, and garlic cloves in a bowl and mix well to combine. Then, set aside.
2. Arrange the chicken wings on a sheet tray. Meanwhile, preheat the oven to 350 degrees.
3. Season the chicken wings with salt, pepper, garlic powder and olive oil. Then, roast in the oven.
4. 15 minutes into the process, glaze the chicken. Do this every 5-7 minutes until the chicken has cooked through.
5. Serve with sliced jalapeños.

NOTE: If you're worried about heat, you can tone it down a bit by adding more brown sugar or honey. Sriracha has a medium heat to it with a really great tangy flavor.

CRISPY CHICKEN *with lime caper sauce*

Yield: *Makes 4 servings* | prep time: *5 minutes* | cook time: *25 minutes*

Ingredients

- 4 medium sized chicken breasts, boneless & skinless
- 1 teaspoon of Kosher salt
- 1 teaspoon of ground black pepper
- 1/2 teaspoon of dried thyme
- 1/2 teaspoon of dried oregano
- 1/2 cup of all purpose flour
- 2 tablespoons of chopped garlic
- 1 cup of vegetable oil
- 1 cup of good white wine
- 2 tablespoons of fresh lime juice
- 2 tablespoons of butter
- 2 tablespoons of capers, drained

"There are million ways to cook chicken breast. You only need to know a few of them. This, however, is one recipe you need in your repertoire!"
-Grandma Pam

1. Preheat an oven proof skillet on the stove until it's hot. Meanwhile, preheat the oven to 400 degrees. Season the chicken with salt, pepper, oregano, and thyme. Then, coat each chicken breast in flour and shake off any excess flour.

2. Add the vegetable oil to the hot skillet. Cook the chicken breasts on one side for 3-4 minutes until golden brown, then flip and place in the oven to finish cooking through. Discard the excess oil before putting the chicken in the oven.

3. When the chicken is done cooking, remove from the oven and set the chicken aside to rest. Meanwhile, place the pan on medium heat on the stove, sauté the garlic for a few moments until fragrant. Then add the white wine, lime juice, and capers to the pan. Sauté for 3-4 minutes.

4. Finish by stirring in the butter to the sauce. Taste and adjust seasonings by adding salt and pepper, if necessary. Pour the sauce over the chicken and serve immediately.

NOTE: It's important to let the chicken breast rest after they come out of the oven. They'll be much juicier this way.

yield: *Makes 4 servings* | prep time: *15 minutes* | cook time: *60 minutes*

Ingredients

-1 roasting chicken (I usually get something between 4 to 6 pounds)
-10 cloves of garlic, finely minced
-1 tablespoon of Kosher salt
-1 tablespoon of ground black pepper
-1 teaspoon of dried basil
-1 teaspoon of dried oregano
-1 teaspoon of dried thyme
-the zest of 1 lemon, finely grated
-4 tablespoons of melted butter

For the root vegetables
Get a mix of anything you like. I typically pick up a few carrots, celery, parsnips, leeks, fennel, and onion. Just cut them into 1 inch pieces.

White Wine Pan Sauce
-1 tablespoon of flour
-1 tablespoon of olive oil
-1 cup of chicken stock
-1 cup of white wine
-salt and pepper to taste

"No matter how many dinner guests you invite, there's always leftover chicken. This one, in particular, makes the best chicken salad!"

-*Grandma Pam*

1. Preheat the oven to 375 degrees.

2. In a large bowl, mix together the minced garlic, salt, pepper, dried basil, dried oregano, dried thyme, lemon zest, and melted butter to form a thick paste.

3. Rub the paste all over the chicken. Pull back the skin and rub some paste between the skin of the chicken and the flesh.

4. Using a roasting rack, place the chicken on the rack and arrange the root vegetables in the bottom of the pan around and under the chicken.

5. Roast the chicken until the internal temperature reaches 165 degrees. This should take about 40-45 minutes.

6. Remove the chicken and the roasted vegetables from the pan and place the pan on the stove over a low to medium flame.

7. Add 1 tablespoon of olive oil to the pan and when it gets hot, add in 1 tablespoon of flour. Stir in the flour and let cook for about 60 seconds.

8. Then, add the chicken stock and white wine and let come to a boil. Then, reduce the heat and let the sauce simmer until it's thickened. Taste and adjust seasoning with salt and pepper if necessary.

NOTE: Be sure to let the chicken come to room temperature before placing it in the hot oven. This will ensure it cooks evenly. It's okay to rub on the seasonings and let the bird sit on a counter in the pan for up to an hour before putting it in the oven.

CHICKEN FRIED SHRIMP *with corn & bacon gravy*

yield: *Makes 3 servings* | prep time: *10 minutes* | cook time: *30 minutes*

Ingredients

-1 pound of jumbo shrimp
(10-12 count per pound),
shelled and deveined
-1 teaspoon of Kosher salt
-1 teaspoon of ground black
pepper
-1/2 teaspoon of garlic powder
-1/2 teaspoon of onion powder
-1 pinch of cayenne pepper
-1 egg, beaten well
-1 cup of buttermilk
-1 tablespoon of hot sauce
-2 cups of flour
-1 cup of cornstarch
-4 cups of vegetable or Canola
oil

Corn & Bacon Gravy
-5 strips of bacon, cut into
small pieces
-1 tablespoon of olive oil
-1/2 cup of minced onion
-2 cloves of garlic, minced
-2 cups of corn kernels (frozen
or fresh)
-1/2 cup of chicken stock
-1 1/2 cups of heavy cream
-salt and pepper to taste

"Let your battered meat rest! Once you coat it, let it sit for a few minutes. You want the batter on the shrimp not in the pan."

-Grandma Pam

1. Season the shrimp with salt, pepper, garlic powder, onion powder, and cayenne. Set aside for a few minutes to marinate. In another bowl, add the buttermilk, hot sauce, and beaten egg.

2. In a third bowl, add together the flour and cornstarch and mix well.

3. Toss the shrimp quickly in the buttermilk, hot sauce, and egg mixture. Then, coat well in the flour cornstarch mixture. Shake off the excess and set the shrimp on a rack for about 10 minutes so the coating can adhere.

4. Meanwhile, preheat the oil to 360 degrees.

5. Fry each shrimp until golden brown. Drain each shrimp on paper towels to absorb any excess oil

6. To make the gravy, sauté the bacon in olive oil with garlic and onion. Once the bacon has cooked through, add the corn and sauté for about 5 minutes more. Then add the corn and bacon mixture to a blender along with the chicken stock and heavy cream. Blend until smooth. Heat the mixture over medium high heat until thickened and season with salt and pepper to taste.

NOTE: This recipe works great with frozen shrimp! For the gravy, never used canned corn or creamed corn. It will change the final flavor profile. Fresh corn is always best. But, when it's not in season, frozen corn comes in a close second.

JERK FRIED CHICKEN *with coconut yam rice*

yield: *Makes 6 servings* | prep time: *15 minutes* | cook time: *20 minutes*

Ingredients

-4 pounds of chicken wings
-2 tablespoons of Jerk spice rub (recipe to follow)
-3 cups of flour
-1 1/2 cups of corn starch
-1 egg, beaten
-8 cups of vegetable or Canola oil

Jerk Spice Rub

-1 tablespoon of garlic powder
-1 teaspoon of cayenne pepper
-2 teaspoons of onion powder
-2 teaspoons of dried parsley
-2 teaspoons of brown sugar
-2 teaspoons of salt
-1 teaspoon of paprika
-1/2 teaspoon of ground allspice
-1 teaspoon of ground black pepper
-1/2 teaspoon of nutmeg
-zest of 2 limes

Combine all ingredients well and store in an air tight container until ready to use.

"Keep lots of the Jerk spice rub on hand. It's great on grilled everything - chicken, fish, beef, pork, and turkey!"
—Grandma Pam

1. Liberally season the chicken wings with the Jerk spice rub.

2. In a separate bowl, combine the cornstarch and flour and set aside.

3. Toss the chicken with the egg and then coat in the flour & cornstarch mixture. Shake off the excess coating and let the chicken wings sit on wire rack for about 10 minutes.

4. Meanwhile, preheat the oil to 360 degrees.

5. When the oil is hot, fry each chicken wing until they're golden brown. Drain the excess oil on paper towels.

NOTE: When frying anything, never over-crowd the pan. If need be, cook in batches. This is your insurance policy that the oil stays hot enough to ensure each chicken wing comes out crispy and not logged with oil.

CHICKEN SAUSAGE *breakfast hash-lettes*

yield: *Makes 4 servings* | prep time: *15 minutes* | cook time: *20 minutes*

Ingredients

Chicken Sausage Patties
-1 pound of ground chicken
-2 teaspoons of brown sugar
-1 teaspoon of Kosher salt
-1 teaspoon of ground black pepper
-1/2 teaspoon of dried sage
-1/2 teaspoon of dried oregano
-1/2 teaspoon of chili powder

-2 tablespoons of olive oil, divided
-1 cup of diced onion
-1 cup of diced bell pepper
-2 pounds of potatoes, diced into 2 inch cubes
-1 cup of shredded cheddar cheese
-1 tablespoon of Kosher salt
-1 tablespoon of ground black pepper

"It's everything you love about an omelette, but without the eggs. Be creative. Toss in whatever you'd like. You can't go wrong with this recipe!"

-Grandma Pam

1. To make the sausage, preheat the oven to 375 degrees.

2. Add the chicken, brown sugar, salt, black pepper, dried sage, dried oregano, and chili powder to a bowl and mix well to combine.

3. Form into 12 1-inch disks and arrange on a sheet tray lined with parchment paper. Roast in the oven for 8-12 minutes, or until cooked through.

4. Meanwhile, in a large bowl, toss together the potatoes, onions, peppers, salt, and pepper until well combined.

5. Arrange on a sheet tray lined with parchment paper and roast in the oven for 10-12 minutes until the potatoes are crispy on the outside.

6. To serve, toss the cooked potatoes and onions with the chicken sausage and top with shredded cheddar cheese.

NOTE: Be sure you're roasting using a sheet tray. You'll need something with low sides so the potatoes crisp up nicely. Also, if you're not using a non-stick pan, invest in parchment paper. If you don't, the starch from the potatoes will stick to the pan. You want to spend your time enjoying the meal, not scraping the pan.

DOUBLE CHEDDAR OX-TAIL *sandwich with sweet lime slaw*

yield: *Makes 4 servings* | **prep time:** *10 minutes* | **cook time:** *10 minutes (Plus 3 hours to braise)*

Ingredients

For the oxtails
- 3 pounds of oxtails
- 1 cup of good red wine
- 1 cup of beef stock
- 2 bay leaves
- 1 medium onion, diced
- 4 cloves of garlic
- 1 medium green bell pepper, diced

For the sandwich
- sliced cheddar cheese
- soft cheddar cheese spread
- ciabatta bun, toasted

For the sweet lime cole slaw
- 2 cups of cole slaw mixed vegetables
- 1/2 cup of mayo
- 1/4 cup of sour cream
- 1 1/2 tablespoons of sugar
- 1/2 teaspoon of garlic powder
- 1/2 teaspoon of onion powder
- 1/2 teaspoon of Kosher salt
- 2 tablespoons of lime juice
- zest of 1 lime

"The smell of the oxtails will be tempting. But, practice discipline and don't open the foil to peek inside. Let them cook undisturbed."
—Grandma Pam

1. Preheat the oven to 400 degrees. Meanwhile, put the ingredients for the oxtails in an oven safe dish and seal it tight with aluminum foil. Cook in the oven for 3 hours, or until the oxtails are super tender.

2. While the oxtails are cooking, prepare the coleslaw by tossing all the ingredients together in a bowl. Then refrigerate until you're ready to assemble the sandwich.

3. Allow the oxtails to cool, then pull the meat from the bones and then put the meat back into the sauce to warm through.

4. To assemble the sandwiches, spread the cheddar cheese spread on the bottom half of the bun. Then, top with the oxtails, the sliced cheddar cheese, and then the coleslaw.

NOTE: Don't have oxtails? No worries! Oxtails can be a bit expensive. This recipe works with other cuts of beef too. Try it with short ribs, London broil, filet mignon, or even pot roast.

LEMON & GARLIC PORK CHOPS

yield: *Makes 4 servings* | **prep time:** *25 minutes* | **cook time:** *10-12 minutes*

Ingredients

- 4 center cut pork chops
- 2 tablespoons of olive oil
- 1 teaspoon of Kosher salt
- 1 teaspoon of black pepper
- 4 cloves of minced garlic
- the zest of 1 lemon
- 1 tablespoon of lemon juice

"You don't want to make anyone sick. It's okay to let the pork chops marinate for up to 20 minutes at room temperature. If you need a longer time, just throw them in to the fridge until you're ready to grill."

-Grandma Pam

1. Place the pork chops in a food storage bag. Toss in all the other ingredients and massage the marinade on the chops. Let the pork chops sit at room temperature for no more than 20 minutes.

2. Then, preheat an in door grill pan.

3. When the grill pan is hot, grill the pork chops on both sides until the internal temperature reaches 160° F.

4. Serve by plating the pork chops and pouring over the pan juices as a sauce.

NOTE: If you're buying super thick pork chops, you can still use this recipe. Just preheat the oven to 400° and after you've grilled one side, flip the chops and put them in the oven. They'll continue cooking through and will be perfect.

HRIMP & GRITS *with bacon butter*

eld: *Makes 4 servings* | prep time: *15 minutes* | cook time: *45 minutes*

Ingredients

For the shrimp
- 1 pound of jumbo shrimp, with the tails on and deveined
- 2 tablespoons of olive oil
- 1/2 tablespoon of salt
- 1/2 tablespoon of pepper
- 1/2 tablespoon of garlic powder

For the grits
- 1 1/2 cups of quick cooking grits
- 3 1/2 cups of chicken stock
- 1 cup of heavy cream
- 1 stick of butter
- 1/2 cup of mascarpone cheese

For the bacon butter
- 5 strips of bacon, cut into small pieces
- 6 tablespoons of butter
- 1/2 teaspoon of black pepper

- fresh herbs, to garnish

"Make sure the grits are cooked thoroughly. Crunchy bacon is good. Crunchy grits are a whole other story!"

—Grandma Pam

1. For the grits, bring the chicken stock to a boil. Then, add the grits. Reduce the heat to medium-low and continue stirring while the grits cook so they don't stick.

2. Once most of the liquid has been absorbed by the grits, they'll be really thick. Add in the butter, heavy cream, and mascarpone cheese and reduce the heat to barely a simmer. Continue stirring occasionally.

3. For the shrimp. Preheat the oven to 400° degrees. Toss the shrimp with the olive oil, salt, pepper, and garlic powder. Arrange on a sheet tray and roast until the shrimp are just barely cooked.

4. Remove the shrimp from the oven and keep them warm on the sheet tray. They'll finish cooking that way.

5. For the bacon butter, cook the bacon on medium heat in a skillet. When the bacon is crispy, remove the bacon fat and keep the bacon in the pan.

6. Add in the butter and black pepper and cook on medium heat for about 30 seconds.

7. To serve, put some grits in a bowl, top them with the shrimp, and drizzle over some bacon butter. Garnish with fresh herbs.

> **NOTE:** You might notice that the grits have gotten too thick before you add in the heavy cream. They're supposed to be that way. When you cook out all the liquid the grits are begging for something more. As soon as you add the heavy cream and mascarpone cheese, they'll get super creamy. This is what you want.

MY GRANNY'S BROWN *bag fried chicken*

yield: *Makes 4 servings* | prep time: *75 minutes* | cook time: *20 minutes*

Ingredients

1 chicken (5-6 pounds) cut into
8 pieces)
1 cup of buttermilk
1/2 cup of hot sauce
1 tablespoon of salt
1 tablespoon of black pepper
1 tablespoon of garlic powder
1/2 tablespoon of chili powder
1 tablespoon of brown sugar
4 cups of all purpose flour
2 cups of corn starch

6-8 cups of vegetable or canola
oil, for frying
Kosher salt for sprinkling

"The longer the chicken sits in the marinade, the better. The acid from the buttermilk tenderizes the chicken. Don't skip this step!"

-Grandma Pam

1. In a large bowl, mix together the hot sauce and buttermilk. Then, add the chicken to the bowl and soak in the buttermilk mixture for at least 1 hour.

2. When you're ready to fry the chicken, remove the chicken from the buttermilk mixture. Then season it liberally with salt, pepper, garlic powder, chili powder, and brown sugar.

3. In a large paper bag, add the flour and cornstarch.

4. Add the chicken to the bag and shake it well to coat each piece of chicken. Remove the chicken and shake off the excess. Place the chicken on a rack for at least 10 minutes so the coating has a chance to adhere.

5. When you're ready, preheat the oil to 360° F. When the oil is hot, fry each piece of chicken until it's golden brown. Drain the excess oil on paper towels, sprinkle with a bit of Kosher salt on each piece, and enjoy the fried chicken while it's still hot.

NOTE: The key to really good crispy chicken is to make sure there's enough moisture on the chicken so the batter can really adhere. This is why soaking the chicken in buttermilk is so important. Also, the reaction from the heat of the oil and the cornstarch causes air pockets to form. These air pockets leave a crunch on the chicken that you won't even believe!

MOTHERED CUBE STEAK *with garlic mashed potatoes*

eld: *Makes 4 servings* | prep time: *10 minutes* | cook time: *40 minutes*

Ingredients

For the cube steak

- 1 pound of cube steak fillets
- 1/2 tablespoon of Kosher salt
- 1/2 tablespoon of black pepper
- 1/2 tablespoon of garlic powder
- 2 cups of all purpose flour
- 3 cups of vegetable oil

For the gravy

- 1/2 cup of diced onion
- 1/2 cup of diced bell pepper
- 1/2 cup of diced celery
- 3 tablespoons of reserved oil
- 3 tablespoons of flour
- 4-5 cups of beef stock

For the mashed potatoes

- 2 pounds of potatoes
- 4 cloves of garlic
- 1 stick of room temperature butter
- 1 tablespoon of salt
- 1 tablespoon of black pepper
- 1/2 tablespoon of granulated garlic
- 3/4 cup of half and half

"Most people are afraid of making homemade gravy. I never knew why. It ain't nothing but some flour and a little stock. Follow my steps below. I know you can do it!"

Grandma Pam

1. To make the cube steak, heat the vegetable oil in a skillet to 360° F.

2. While the oil is heating, season the cube steaks with salt, pepper, and garlic powder. Dust them in flour and then shake off the excess.

3. Fry the cube steaks until they're golden brown, then set them on paper towels to drain.

4. Meanwhile, pour off the excess oil, leaving about 3 tablespoons in the pan. Sauté the onion, bell pepper, and celery until they're just tender. Then sprinkle in the flour and cook it until it's brown while stirring often. This should take about 5-6 minutes.

5. Stir in the beef stock and bring the mixture to a boil, then reduce it to just above a simmer. Add the cube steaks and cook for another 10 minutes.

6. For the mashed potatoes, boil the potatoes in water with the garlic cloves until they're fork tender. Then, drain them well and mix with butter, salt, pepper, granulated garlic, and pour in the half and half until the desired consistency is reached.

> **NOTE:** The key to smooth mashed potatoes is to mash in the butter and seasonings first. Once the potatoes are smooth, then add in the half and half gradually. You shouldn't mind a few lumps, but if you like a smoother finished product, never add the liquid first.

The Blue Ribbon Meat Market

Growing up with my Granny was an experience. There were things that we did just because. Now that I think about it, today, they don't make much since. But, when I was growing up through these times, these things were like a science. Let's take Saturdays for example. That was the national day of chores in my Granny's house. It just was. No kid had to go to school and no adult had to go to work. So, everyone was home and accounted for. As our feet hit the floor and we said our good mornings, the routines would start. We'd make our beds or in this case, fold the covers and sheets because we either slept on the floor or the couch. My Granny was a coffee drinker, so I'd smell the coffee brewing. She always had a can of that stuff. She liked it with just sugar. She drank it every day. Between that and the wood cleaner in the yellow can for the wood tables, the smell became more and more familiar. Or, maybe it was the ammonia from the blue glass cleaner. If this were the time of the month where there was more month than money, you'd have to grab some water and a piece of newspaper to clean the glass on the coffee table. You had to put in a little bit more elbow grease, but you could still get the glass clean. We started by removing the candy dish. It was always filled with nuts and peppermints. Granny would sometimes buy the mixed candy with the orange butterscotch. That would always be left over; no one liked that flavor at all.

One of the events I looked forward to the most was going to the meat market. To this day, I still don't know why I loved the idea so much. I think maybe it was because we were going to do stuff. You know, there was a sense of purpose. Blue Ribbon Meat Market was our store. We would walk in and there was a scent that would overtake you. It was okay though because even at 9 years old, I was able to deal with it. It was like another language. It seemed all you heard were women shouting, "I'll take 3 dollars worth of leg quarters!" or "Give me 7 dollars worth of pork chops!" You see, pounds and ounces weren't a form a measure. When you grow up in the hood like I did, with our socio-economic status, you ordered things based on the amount of cash in your pocket. Sometimes, that cash wasn't much.

My grandmother would take her number from the ticket machine and when it was called, she'd order her meat. "I'll take 8 dollars worth of chicken - white and dark, please!" she'd say.

They'd reach into the glass, grab the unending supply of chicken, and weigh it until the machine read slightly less than $8. Sometimes, they'd play this game where they'd remove one piece of chicken because it was way more than $8. It came out to like $8 and a quarter. The white guy with the apron would ask my Granny, "Is this okay, ma'am?" She'd reply, "Sure, that's fine." She'd reach into her trench coat that she bought from Montgomery Ward's, hand the guy her hard earned cash. He'd give her the change and hand her the bag. She immediately gave the bag to me without missing a beat. It was as if she had said, "I paid for it. You carry it." I grabbed the bag with a smile as we walked out the door and back to Granny's house.

MOTHERED CHICKEN *pot pie*

eld: *Makes 6 servings* | prep time: *30 minutes* | cook time: *45 minutes*

Ingredients

For the crust
2 cups of flour

1 stick of cold butter, cut into pieces

1 teaspoon of salt

6 to 8 tablespoons of ice cold water

For the chicken
-4 chicken thighs, boneless & skinless, cut into bite sized pieces

-1 teaspoon of salt

-1 teaspoon of pepper

-1/2 teaspoon of garlic powder

-1 cup of flour

-1 cup of cornstarch

-1 egg, beaten

-4 to 6 cups of vegetable oil, for frying

For the gravy
-2 tablespoons of flour

-2 cups of chicken stock

-2 cups of beef stock

-1/2 cup of onion, diced

-1/2 cup of bell pepper, diced

-1/2 cup of celery, diced

-1 cup of frozen peas & carrots

-egg wash (1 egg beaten with a bit of water)

"Don't worry! If making the homemade crust scares you a bit, a store bought crust will work, too."

-Grandma Pam

1. To make the crust, mix the flour, butter, and salt together until the butter is well incorporated. Then, add the water tablespoon by tablespoon until the crust just comes together. Form it into a ball, wrap it in plastic wrap and chill until you're ready to use.

2. For the chicken, preheat the oil to 360° F. Season the chicken with salt, pepper, and garlic powder in one bowl. In a separate bowl, mix together the cornstarch and flour.

3. To coat the chicken, dip in the egg mixture, dredge in the flour mixture, shake off the excess, and then fry until golden brown. Drain on paper towels when done.

4. For the gravy, pour off the excess oil, leaving about 3 tablespoons in the pan. Sauté the onion, bell pepper, and celery until they're just tender. Then sprinkle in the flour and cook it until it's brown while stirring often. This should take about 5-6 minutes.

5. Stir in the stock and bring the mixture to a boil, then reduce it to just above a simmer. Add the chicken and the peas & carrots. Mix well.

6. Preheat the oven to 375 degrees. Roll out the dough. Add the filling to the pan and top it with the dough. Brush on the egg wash and bake until golden brown.

NOTE: The great thing about this recipe is that it freezes well. Do everything up to step #6. Then, just wrap the whole thing tightly and store it in the freezer for up to a week. When you're ready, egg wash it (while it's still frozen) and bake it in the oven. It'll take about 40 minutes at 350°.

BROWN SUGAR *rubbed salmon with black olive tapenade*

Yield: *Makes 2 servings* | prep time: *3 minutes* | cook time: *15 minutes*

Ingredients

For the salmon
- 2 6oz salmon steaks or fillets
- 1/2 tablespoon of Kosher salt
- 1/2 tablespoon of black pepper
- 2 tablespoons of brown sugar
- 1/2 teaspoon of garlic powder
- 1/2 teaspoon of smoked paprika
- 2 tablespoons of olive oil

For the tapenade
- 1 medium garlic clove
- 2 teaspoons of capers
- 2 cups of black olives, pitted
- 1 tablespoon of lemon juice
- 2 tablespoons of olive oil
- a pinch of salt
- a pinch of black pepper

- 1 lemon

"I love using salmon steaks for this. Ask your fishmonger to cut you a few steaks for this recipe. If you're only able to find fillets, don't stress. Those will work, too!"

—Grandma Pam

1. Preheat the oven to 400 degrees. Meanwhile, also get a cast iron skillet hot by placing it over a medium high flame on the stove for 3 minutes.

2. In a bowl, combine the salt, pepper, brown sugar, garlic powder, smoked paprika, and olive oil into a paste. Rub it all over the salmon. When ready, place the salmon in the skillet and don't touch it for at least 90 seconds. When it pulls away easily, flip it and put it in the oven to continue cooking.

3. For the tapenade, chop the garlic, capers, and black olives until they're really fine and almost ground. Add the ingredients to a bowl and then loosen the tapenade by adding the lemon juice, olive oil, a pinch of salt, and a pinch of pepper.

4. To serve, remove the salmon from the oven and top with some of tapenade and fresh squeeze of lemon.

> **NOTE:** Not a fan of salmon, no worries. This same process works with any type of fatty fish.
> You know, even chicken thighs or pork chops would be good with this too!

CHORIZO BURGER *with sautéed shrimp & chipotle mayo*

yield: *Makes 3 servings* | prep time: *15 minutes* | cook time: *25 minutes*

Ingredients

For the burger
1 pound of ground chorizo
1 teaspoon of minced garlic
1 tablespoon of minced onion
1/2 teaspoon of black pepper
2 tablespoons of olive oil

For the shrimp
12 jumbo shrimp, cleaned &
deveined
1 teaspoon of Old Bay seasoning
1/2 teaspoon of Kosher salt
2 tablespoons of olive oil

For the chipotle mayo
1 cup of good mayo
1 chipotle pepper in adobo
1 tablespoon of adobo sauce
1 teaspoon of sugar
1 pinch of salt

3 Brioche buns, toasted
cilantro, to garnish

"These burgers are messy, but good. Have extra napkins ready. Also, let me remind you how important it is to let the burgers rest when they come out of skillet. You want the juice in the burger… not on your plate!"

—Grandma Pam

1. In a large bowl, mix together the chorizo, minced garlic, minced onion, and black pepper. Form into 3 patties. Meanwhile, heat a skillet and then add the olive oil.

2. Cook the burgers on both sides until they've cooked through. Meanwhile, season the shrimp with the Old Bay seasoning, Kosher salt, and olive oil.

3. Remove the burgers and let them rest. In the same skillet, sauté the shrimp until they're just done.

4. To make the chipotle mayo, mince the chipotle pepper. To make it less spicy, remove the seeds before mincing. Then, mix together with the mayo, adobo, sugar, and salt. Refrigerate until you're ready to use.

5. To assemble the burgers, spread the chipotle mayo on both pieces of the toasted bun. Then layer the chorizo patty, cilantro, and sautéed shrimp.

NOTE: Not a fan of chorizo? No big deal. Use ground chicken, ground pork, ground beef, ground turkey, or even ground lamb will work. Feeling exotic? Mix them all together and make the burger. It'll be delish!

CORNMEAL CRUSTED *pork chops*

yield: *Makes 4 servings* | prep time: *10 minutes* | cook time: *20 minutes*

Ingredients

4 center cut pork chops
1 teaspoon of salt
1 teaspoon of pepper
1 teaspoon of garlic powder
1 teaspoon of smoked paprika
1 cup of cornmeal
2 cups of flour
1/2 cup of hot sauce
1 egg beaten
1 cup of buttermilk

3-4 cups of vegetable oil, for frying

"I do understand budgets. So, if center cut pork chops aren't on sale, don't get them. Buy the kind that are on sale. They'll be just as tasty!"

-Grandma Pam

1. In a large bowl, combine the hot sauce, beaten egg, and buttermilk. Marinate the pork chops in the liquid for at least 2 hours. Overnight is always better. Then take them out without patting them dry and liberally season with salt, pepper, garlic powder, and smoked paprika.

2. In another bowl, combine the cornmeal and flour together. Dredge each pork chop in the mixture and shake off the excess. Let the dredged pork chops sit for a few minutes. Meanwhile, heat the oil in a deep skillet to 360 degrees.

3. Fry each chop until golden brown on both sides. Do this in 2 batches so as not to overcrowd the pan.

4. Remove the chops from the oil and drain them on paper towels to remove the excess oil.

NOTE: Cornmeal is great for dredging proteins like pork chops. However, don't go overboard. Too much cornmeal and the crust becomes a crunchy grainy mess. That's why it's important to mix the cornmeal with flour. You'll get just the right texture you're looking for!

CHICKEN MEATLOAF *with tomato ketchup glaze*

yield: *Makes 6 servings* | prep time: *15 minutes* | cook time: *30 minutes*

Ingredients

- 2 pounds of ground chicken
- 3 slices of white bread (crust removed)
- 1 cup of buttermilk
- 1/2 cup of grated onion
- 3 cloves of minced garlic
- 1/2 cup of grated green bell pepper
- 1/2 cup of grated celery
- 1 tablespoon of salt
- 1 tablespoon of pepper
- 1/2 tablespoon of onion powder
- 3 tablespoons of olive oil
- 1/2 tablespoon of paprika
- 1 pinch of chili flakes

For the glaze
- 2 cups of ketchup
- a few dashes of Worcestershire
- 1 cup of brown sugar

"Chicken works really well with this recipe. But, it' it's not on sale, don't stress. Any type of ground meat will work!"

—Grandma Pam

1. Preheat the oven to 375 degrees. Also, add the bread to a bowl and pour in the buttermilk to soften to bread.

2. Meanwhile, in a large bowl, combine the ground chicken, onion, garlic, bell pepper, celery, salt, pepper, onion powder, paprika, olive oil and chili flakes. Mix well and then add the softened bread. You can discard any buttermilk that didn't get absorbed in the bread.

3. Form meatloaf into a baking dish and bake for 25-30 minutes or until the internal temperature reaches 160 degrees.

4. To make the glaze, mix the ketchup with the brown sugar and Worcestershire sauce and pour on top of the meatloaf about 10 minutes before it's done cooking.

5. Once the meatloaf is done cooking, let it rest for about 10 minutes before cutting into it. This will ensure each bite is moist and juicy.

NOTE: Whatever cut of meat you decide to use, don't forget that it's important to use bread that's been soaked in buttermilk. This is the insurance policy that your meatloaf is moist and juicy…not a hockey puck.

COLLARD GREEN *and cornbread cake*

yield: Makes 8 servings | prep time: 15 minutes | cook time: 45 minutes

Ingredients

For the cornbread
- 1 cup of cornmeal
- 1 cup of flour
- 1 cup of sugar
- 2 tablespoons of baking powder
- 1 teaspoon of salt
- 1 stick of melted butter
- 2 eggs
- 3/4 cup of buttermilk

For the gravy
- 2 tablespoons of flour
- 2 tablespoons of vegetable oil
- 2 cups of chicken stock
- 2 cups of beef stock

For the fried chicken
Use the recipe in this book "My Granny's Brown Bag Fried Chicken"

Mashed Potato Frosting
- 2 pounds of potatoes, boiled, drained and cooled
- 1 stick of room temperature butter
- 1 tablespoon of salt
- 1 tablespoon of black pepper
- 1/2 tablespoon of granulated garlic
- 1/3 cup of half and half

- Sautéed collard greens

"If you need a cute idea to present something new for any occasion, this is it. Just remember, for the best results, assemble at the last possible moment!"

—Grandma Pam

1. For the cornbread, preheat the oven to 375 degrees. In a large bowl, mix together the cornmeal, flour, sugar, salt, and baking powder. Stir in the butter, eggs, melted butter, an buttermilk until smooth. Pour into two 9-inch round baking pans and bake until golden brown and set in the center. This should take about 18-20 minutes.

2. Remove the cornbread and let cool. Meanwhile, to make the greens, just sauté in olive oil until tender and then season with salt and pepper. Be sure to drain the liquid from the collard greens.

3. For the gravy, cook the flour and vegetable oil together until the mixture becomes brown. Then, whisk in the chicken stock and beef stock. Once the gravy comes to a boil, reduce the heat to just above a simmer until you're ready to serve.

4. For the mashed potato frosting, mix together the potatoes, butter, salt, pepper, and garlic until the potatoes are smooth. Then, add the half and half until the desired consistency is reached.

5. To assemble the cake, put the sautéed greens in between each layer of cornbread. Then, using the mashed potatoes cover the outside of the cake. Garnish with fried chicken and drizzle with gravy.

NOTE: Making the collard greens are easy. Just pick up a bag of frozen collards and sauté them with salt and pepper in olive oil. Then, be sure to drain them really well before putting them in between the cornbread layers!

PECAN CRUSTED CATFISH

Yield: *Makes 4 servings* | prep time: *10 minutes* | cook time: *10 minutes*

Ingredients

- 2 cups of pecans, finely ground
- 2 cup of cornmeal
- 4 cups of vegetable oil, for frying
- 4 catfish fillets
- 1 1/2 teaspoons of salt
- 1 tablespoon of black pepper
- 1 teaspoon of garlic powder
- 1/2 cup of buttermilk

"The ground pecans add a sweet and nutty flavor to the fish. It's a perfect balance. Remember, don't have the flame too high. You don't want to burn the pecans before the fish is cooked through!"

Grandma Pam

1. In a large bowl, pour the buttermilk over the fish. Then, season the fish with salt, pepper, and garlic powder.
2. In another bowl, combine the cornmeal and ground pecans until they're well mixed. Then, dredge the fish in the cornmeal and pecan mixture and set aside for a few moments to the coating can adhere really well to the fish.
3. Preheat the vegetable oil to 360 degrees. Then, fry the fish fillets on both sides until they're golden brown.
4. When the fish fillets are done, remove them and set them on paper towels to drain.

NOTE: Can't find catfish in your area? Try tilapia, perch, grouper, or even cod will work just fine for this recipe. Actually, any mild flavored white fish will work fine!

PULLED JERK *chicken sliders*

Yield: *Makes 6 servings* | prep time: *10 minutes* | cook time: *2 hours*

Ingredients

For the Jerk BBQ sauce
- 4 cups of chicken stock
- 1 cup of chopped onion
- 2 cups of green onion, chopped
- 2 tablespoons of minced ginger
- 1 jalapeño pepper, minced
- 1/2 cup of molasses
- 1/2 cup of brown sugar
- 1 tablespoon of ground allspice
- 1 teaspoon of ground nutmeg
- 1 teaspoon of ground cinnamon
- 1 teaspoon of ground thyme
- 2 tablespoons of soy sauce
- 1 can of dark beer
- 2 cups of tomato ketchup

- soft potato rolls
- 4 chicken breast, boneless & skinless
- 2 tablespoons of olive oil
- 1 teaspoon of black pepper
- cilantro, to garnish

"Make the BBQ sauce in advance. Then, all you'd need to do is roast the chicken - which takes a short period of time. Before you know it, you'll be chowing down to a meal that transports you to the Caribbean!"

—Grandma Pam

1. To make the Jerk BBQ sauce, combine all the ingredients in a sauce pan and cook on medium low heat for 2 hours until thick. Remove from the heat and allow to cool.

2. For the chicken, preheat the oven to 375 degrees. Drizzle each chicken breast with olive oil and black pepper. Then, place on a sheet tray and roast until the chicken breasts have cooked through.

3. While the chicken breasts are still warm, use two forks to pull at each chicken breast until the meat is shredded. Toss the shredded meat with as much Jerk BBQ sauce as desired, then serve by piling the chicken on a bun and top with fresh cilantro.

NOTE: Swap out your normal BBQ sauce for this recipe. It goes great on all things that you'd normally grill or roast in the oven. It's a distinct taste that's full of flavor and will have you licking your fingers after each bite!

Fried Turkey: I Did It First!

I had seen my Grandmother fry chicken a gazillion times. I was 9 years old. Or, maybe I was 10. Either way, when you've seen something so many times, it doesn't matter that you've never done it before, you think you know how to do it. I had seen the way it worked. My grandmother would take the shortening and spoon it out of the canister into the large cast iron skillet. While it was getting hot, she'd put seasoned salt and black pepper on the chicken wings. That's all the seasoning she used. She'd then pour the flour in the bag. Once she felt she had enough flour in the bag, she'd fold the wings into that triangle shape and toss them in the bag. She'd shake the bag real good so each wing was coated with the flour. Then, she'd put one hand on her hip while she placed each wing into the hot oil. The hand on her hip thing was important. It added a certain je ne sais quoi to the chicken. You know, I really can't describe what it added to the finished product, but she did it so many times that I thought it was part of the process. So, when I fried chicken, I did it too.

I was home alone and feeling very motivated, as I normally am. I pulled the wings from the fridge, seasoned them with seasoned salt and pepper, just the way my grandmother did. I saw her do it so many times that I could feel when enough seasoning was on the chicken. I found a paper bag and loaded it with flour. I shook the chicken in it and then I put my hand on my hip. At that age, I didn't have a hip. So, I placed my hand on the side of my stomach. It was the next best thing. I placed each wing into the hot oil until each wing was golden brown. As I flipped the chicken, it looked beautiful. I knew I was on to something. I got a bit cocky because I had just replicated my grandmother's fried chicken recipe.

When my grandmother came home, she asked what I had done. I told her I had fried chicken. Imagine my surprise when she said we didn't have any chicken in the house and wondered how I could have done so. It was as if everything I had just done was a dream...no, a nightmare. I began to retrace my steps. I took out the wings. I seasoned them. I folded them. I floured them. I put my hand on the side of my stomach. I flipped them when they were golden brown. Yes, I fried chicken. My grandmother looked at me and told me those were actually turkey wings. Imagine my surprise. I laugh at it now, but the truth is that I guess I was frying turkey long before it even became popular.

CHICKEN FRIED TURKEY *with cornbread waffles*

yield: *Makes 4 servings* | prep time: *20 minutes* | cook time: *20 minutes*

Ingredients

For the fried turkey
-4, 6 ounce portions of turkey breast, pounded thin
-2 teaspoons of Kosher salt
-2 teaspoons of ground black pepper
-1 teaspoon of onion powder
-2 teaspoons of chili powder
-1 teaspoon of cayenne pepper
-1/4 cup of good hot sauce
-2 teaspoons of brown sugar
-2 cups of flour
-1 cup of cornstarch
-4 cups of vegetable oil, for frying

For the waffles
-1 cup of flour
-1 cup of sugar
-1 cup of cornmeal
-2 eggs
-1 stick of melted butter
-3 tablespoons of baking powder
-1 teaspoon of salt
-1 1/4 cup of buttermilk

"You ever get a craving for holiday food, but it's not the holiday? This dish is sure to quench that thirst. It's fun to make and even more fun to eat!"

—Grandma Pam

1. In a bowl, combine the salt, black pepper, onion powder, chili powder, cayenne, brown sugar, and hot sauce together. Then, massage the mixture on the turkey breasts and let stand at room temperature for about 20 minutes. Meanwhile, preheat the oil in a skillet to about 360 degrees.

2. In another bowl, combine the cornstarch and flour together. Then, dredge the turkey breasts in the flour mixture and shake off the excess. Fry in the oil on both sides until golden brown.

3. For the waffles, preheat a waffle maker. Then, in a large bowl, mix together the flour, sugar, cornmeal, eggs, melted butter, baking powder, salt, and buttermilk until smooth.

4. After oiling the waffle maker, add about 1/4 to 1/2 cup of batter to the waffle maker and cook until the waffles are done.

5. Serve waffles and chicken fried turkey with cranberry & orange relish.

NOTE: Sometimes turkey breasts are hard to find, especially the fresh ones. If you find some in your local supermarket, grab them for this recipe. But, if you can't find them, that's okay. You can use pork chops or chicken breasts!

White Beans, Rice, and Cornbread (Made from the Blue Box)

There was a period of time that I lived with my mother. There were so many ups and downs during those times that it's now a blur. I still hold on to a lot of memories during those times. There were some very good times. Then, there were some not so good times. All of the in-between is where I get foggy. My mother isn't a bad person. I just don't think she was prepared to deal with what it meant to raise a son in the urban streets of Chicago. There were some things that I can only assume she did out of instinct. As a matter of fact, I do believe it was instinct because I saw so much of my grandmother in some of the things my mother did. It wasn't exactly the things she did, but it was more about how she did them. There were similarities.

For example, most Saturdays held the same routines. I would hear Marvin Gaye or Stevie Wonder or Chaka Kahn or Gladys Knight and I knew what time it was. It was time to handle some household chores. You know, the deep cleaning stuff that you just couldn't get to during the weekday. For a long while, there was just the two of us - my mother and I. But, you'd think we had an army coming over. She cooked so much food that we would eat holiday food for a week after the holiday had passed. This was how it was every holiday. There were things that just happened out of routine and I thought this was one of them.

One of my mother's go-to meals was a dish with stewed white beans. I can't really explain it. Well, let me try. She would start with a few ham hocks. This was before the days of smoked turkey and meat substitutes were popular in Southern style cooking. Then, she used to soak the dried white beans overnight. To this day, I never knew what that accomplished. I tried cooking them both ways, so I can't tell the difference. I think this is because this is how my grandmother cooked them. She would drain the soaked beans and boil them with the ham hocks. I get foggy on the seasonings she used, but somehow I remember some type of seasoned salt, the white canister of black pepper, and a few bay leaves always made it into the pot. I do remember her cutting an onion to two, too. She didn't add garlic though. I'm not sure why.

To accompany the beans there was always a pan of cornbread. Again, I don't know why. That's just the way it was. I suppose a nice baguette, crispy crostini, or soft focaccia could have done it. But, alas, we had cornbread. It wasn't the stuff made from scratch either. It was the stuff that was in the blue box. That's what we had - the blue box cornbread. If you're reading this and you're from the 'hood, you know exactly what I'm referring to. To go along the blue box cornbread and the white beans that were soaked overnight was chicken. Not just any chicken either, but fried chicken. That was the unspoken rule. You had to have the soaked white beans over rice, the blue box cornbread, and the fried chicken. This was the way it was supposed to go. I don't know why, but it was.

MY MAMA'S SKILLET CHICKEN *with white bean puree*

yield: *Makes 6 servings* | prep time: *10 minutes* | cook time: *45 minutes*

Ingredients

For the chicken
- 1 whole chicken, cut up
- 1 tablespoon of salt
- 1 teaspoon of pepper
- 1/2 teaspoon of red pepper flakes
- 1 tablespoon of brown sugar
- 1/2 tablespoon of garlic powder
- 1/2 tablespoon of dried rosemary
- 1/2 cup of olive oil

For the white bean puree
- 1 tablespoon of butter
- 1 tablespoon of olive oil
- 1 cup of minced onion
- 1 garlic clove, minced
- 1 sprig of thyme
- 1 sprig of rosemary
- 2 15 ounce cans of white beans, drained and rinsed
- 2 cups of chicken stock
- salt and pepper to taste

"This chicken recipe is so easy to make. You basically season it and let the oven do all the work. For a really good outcome, roast your chicken in a cast iron skillet. It makes all the difference in the world!"
—Grandma Pam

1. Preheat the oven to 400 degrees. Meanwhile, in a bowl, mix together the salt, pepper, red pepper flakes, brown sugar, garlic powder, dried rosemary, and olive oil to form a thick paste. Rub, the paste all over the pieces of chicken and arrange on a sheet tray.

2. Roast the chicken in the oven until the outside is crispy and the inside is tender and moist. This takes about 20-25 minutes.

3. Meanwhile, to start on the white bean puree, sauté the minced onion and garlic in the olive oil and butter until the onions are translucent. Then, add the chicken stock, thyme, rosemary and white beans. Cook for about 20 minutes on medium heat until the liquid has reduced by over half.

4. Then, discard the rosemary and thyme sprigs and puree the mixture in a blender until smooth. Season with salt and pepper to taste.

5. Serve the chicken and white bean puree warm.

> **NOTE:** You'll notice that there are a variety of canned white beans in the supermarket. Get the white beans that are on sale! They all pretty much taste the same.

6-HOUR WINE BRAISED *short ribs with crispy onions*

yield: *Makes 6 servings* | prep time: *20 minutes* | cook time: *6 hours*

Ingredients

For the short ribs
- 5 pounds of short ribs
- 1 bottle of good red wine
- 2 cups of chopped onion
- 1 cup of chopped celery
- 1 cup of chopped bell pepper
- 10 garlic cloves, smashed
- 1 cup of beef stock
- 2 bay leaves
- 1 tablespoon of salt
- 1 teaspoon of pepper
- 1 1/2 tablespoons of cornstarch
- 1 1/2 tablespoons of cold water

For the crispy onions
- 1 onion, cut into thin rings
- 1 teaspoon of salt
- 1/2 teaspoon of pepper
- 1/2 teaspoon of Cajun seasoning
- 1 cup of flour
- 3 cups of vegetable oil, for frying

"Some would say to sear the short ribs first. I'll go on record and say that it does nothing for the taste of the short ribs in the end. My method always works - just drop them into the pan, cover them tightly, and they'll come out perfect every time!"

–Grandma Pam

1. Preheat the oven to 350 degrees. Add the short ribs to an oven safe dish and season with salt and pepper. Then, pour in the red wine and beef stock. Top the short ribs with the onions, celery, and bell pepper. Tuck the garlic and the bay leaves between the short ribs, cover with aluminum foil, and bake in the oven for 4 hours.

2. After 3 hours, take the short ribs out of the oven. In a bowl, mix together the cornstarch and water until it's smooth. Then pour that into the sauce that's formed around the short ribs. Cover tightly with aluminum foil and cook for about 90 minutes.

3. For the crispy onions, preheat the oil to 360 degrees.

4. Season the onions with salt, pepper, and Cajun seasoning. Then, coat in flour and fry until golden brown. Drain on paper towels to remove excess oil and use to garnish the short ribs.

NOTE: These short ribs beg to be served over something creamy and delicious. Roasted sweet potato grits usually do the trick. Just roast a sweet potato until it's super tender and then stir it into creamy grits with a bit of heavy cream and mascarpone cheese!

CRISPY PECAN *crusted shrimp*

yield: *Makes 4 servings* | prep time: *10 minutes* | cook time: *10 minutes*

Ingredients

- 2 cups of pecans, finely ground
- 2 cups of flour
- 4 cups of vegetable oil, for frying
- 1 pound of jumbo shrimp, cleaned and deveined
- 1 1/2 teaspoons of salt
- 1 tablespoon of black pepper
- 1 teaspoon of garlic powder
- 1/2 cup of buttermilk

"Shrimp can be expensive, but worth it. If you're going to cook shrimp, go for the jumbo shrimp. They're sweeter and juicier. You can use frozen or fresh; they'll both work with this recipe!"

-Grandma Pam

1. In a large bowl, pour the buttermilk over the shrimp. Then, season the shrimp with salt, pepper, and garlic powder.
2. In another bowl, combine the flour and ground pecans until they're well mixed. Then, dredge the shrimp in the flour and pecan mixture and set aside for a few moments to the coating can adhere really well to the fish.
3. Preheat the vegetable oil to 360 degrees. Then, fry the shrimp on both sides until they're golden brown.
4. When the shrimp are done, remove them and set them on paper towels to drain.

> **NOTE:** You never want to overcook shrimp. They'll turn to an awful rubbery texture. Cook them just until they're done and let the carryover heat finish the cooking for you. That's your insurance policy for juicy succulent shrimp every time!

RAINBOW CANDY *glazed chicken*

yield: *Makes 8 servings* | prep time: *5 minutes* | cook time: *40 minutes*

Ingredients

- 1 medium sized chicken, about 4-5 pounds
- 1 individual sized pack of rainbow candies
- 2 tablespoons of water
- 1 tablespoon of grated onion
- 1 tablespoon of grated garlic
- 1/2 teaspoon of salt
- 1/2 teaspoon of pepper
- 1 tablespoon of whole grain mustard
- a few dashes of Worcestershire sauce
- 1/2 cup of brown sugar
- 1/2 stick of butter
- 1 pinch of all spice
- 1 pinch of red pepper flakes
- lemons, to garnish

"If you're looking for another way to cook chicken, this is it. It's sweet. It's spicy. It's sticky. It's super easy to cook which makes it perfect for a weeknight treat!"

—Grandma Pam

1. Preheat the oven to 375 degrees. Spread the chicken out on a baking sheet lined with parchment paper and put it in the oven to roast for 15 minutes.

2. Meanwhile, to make the glaze, melt the rainbow candies in with the water over medium heat in a saucepan. Then, add all of the other ingredients - grated onion, grated garlic, salt, pepper, whole grain mustard, Worcestershire sauce, brown sugar, butter, red pepper flakes, and allspice. Cook the glaze over medium heat until it thickens slightly.

3. After the chicken has roasted for 15 minutes, remove it from the oven and brush on a layer of glaze every 5 minutes until it's cooked through. The internal temperature should reach 160 degrees.

4. Finish by adding a squeeze of fresh lemon juice over the chicken. Enjoy while it's hot.

NOTE: The rainbow candies are loaded with sugar. This could cause a mess when roasting the chicken, so be sure you're using parchment paper. This will save you tons of time when it's time to clean up and wash the dishes.

BRAISED COLLARD GREEN *fettuccine with smoked turkey "bacon"*

yield: *Makes 4 servings* | prep time: *10 minutes* | cook time: *25 minutes*

Ingredients

-1 cup of smoked turkey, chopped
-1/2 pound of fettuccine, cooked and drained
-1/4 cup of olive oil
-1 teaspoon of minced garlic
-1 teaspoon of minced shallots
-1 tablespoon of butter
-1/4 cup of good white wine
-1 cup of cooked collard greens, chopped
-1 cup of heavy cream
-1/2 cup of grated Parmesan cheese
-fresh black pepper, to garnish

"I always make way too many collard greens. This is a great way to repurpose them into a fantastic recipe. The best thing about this is that it uses a leftover pot of greens!"

—Grandma Pam

1. Heat the olive oil and butter in a large skillet until the butter is fully melted. Then, sauté the shallots, smoked turkey, and garlic together for a few minutes until they're fragrant.

2. Then, add in the white wine and let it reduce by half. Then, add in the heavy cream.

3. Once the heavy cream reduces and thickens a bit, fold in the collard greens and let them heat through. Then, toss with the cooked pasta.

4. Sprinkle in the Parmesan cheese. To serve, garnish with fresh black pepper.

NOTE: If you're in a hurry and you need the cream sauce to thicken right away, skip the first part of step #3 above. Instead, mix together 1 teaspoon of cornstarch with 1 teaspoon of cold water and pour that into the cream sauce. Once it boils, it'll thicken right away.

STEAK FAJITA PITAS

yield: *Makes 4 servings* | prep time: *20 minutes* | cook time: *10 minutes*

Ingredients

For the steak
-2 8 ounce rib eye steaks
-1 tablespoon of salt
-1 teaspoon of pepper
-1/2 teaspoon of cumin
-1/2 teaspoon of chili powder
-1/4 teaspoon of garlic powder
-1/4 teaspoon of onion powder
-1 teaspoon of brown sugar
-1/2 teaspoon of red pepper flakes
-2 tablespoons of olive oil

Suggested Condiments
-chopped lime
-prepared guacamole
-sautéed onions and peppers
-fresh cilantro
-fresh pita bread

"The key to a good steak is to let it get really crusty on one side before flipping it. You must, and I do mean must, resist the urge to flip the steaks over before it's time. Also, after the steaks are done, let them rest before cutting. They'll stay juicier that way!"

Grandma Pam

1. In a bowl, combine the salt, pepper, cumin, chili powder, garlic powder, onion powder, brown sugar, and red pepper flakes. Mix well. Then add the olive oil and make a paste. Rub that paste on the rib eye steaks and let them sit at room temperature for at least 20 minutes.

2. In the meantime, preheat a grill pan until it's smoking hot. Then, add the rib eye steaks to the pan. Don't touch them. Let them cook on one side for 3 minutes.

3. After the steaks have cooked on one side, flip them over and cook them to your desired doneness.

4. Once the steaks have finished cooking, set them aside and let them rest for at least 7 minutes before slicing them to serve.

NOTE: Rib eyes work really well for this recipe because they're naturally tender and juicy. But, if there's another cut of steak that you like, use the same process, just switch out the steak. The flavor profile is so versatile that it'll work with any cut of meat!

PUTTANESCA *chicken fettuccine*

yield: *Makes 2 servings* | prep time: 5 *minutes* | cook time: 15 *minutes*

Ingredients

- 1/2 pound of cooked fettuccine
- 2 cups of leftover chicken, diced
- 2 tablespoons of capers
- 1 tablespoon of garlic, minced
- 1/2 cup of pitted black olives
- 3/4 cup of good olive oil
- 1 cup of cherry tomatoes
- 1/2 teaspoon of dried oregano
- 1/2 teaspoon of dried basil
- 1/2 teaspoon of Kosher salt
- 1/2 teaspoon of black pepper
- 1 pinch of red pepper flakes

"After I'm done making roast chicken, I typically need a good recipe that uses the leftover chicken in a really great way. This recipe does the trick. A rotisserie chicken works just as well, too!"

—Grandma Pam

1. In a skillet, heat the olive oil and sauté the garlic, chicken, tomatoes, capers, and olives together for about 3-4 minutes until the chicken is heated through.

2. Season the sauce with salt, pepper, dried basil, and dried oregano. Add a pinch of red pepper flakes.

3. After the sauce cooks for 2-3 minutes more, toss with the cooked pasta and serve. Be sure to mix well to combine all the ingredients.

NOTE: This is one of those recipes where you're totally allowed to break all of the rules. If you like a different pasta, switch it out. If you like different veggies, switch them out. In the end, it's about the flavors that make you palate dance!

desserts and all things sweet!

CHOCOLATE HAZELNUT *mini tarts*

yield: *Makes 8 servings* | prep time: *20 minutes* | cook time: *5 minutes*

Ingredients

For the crust
-24 cream-filled chocolate wafer cookies
-1 stick of melted butter
-1 pinch of salt

For the filling
-1 cup of chocolate hazelnut spread
-4 ounces of cream cheese
-1/2 cup of powdered sugar
-1 cup of heavy cream
-1 teaspoon of vanilla extract

-chocolate sauce, to garnish

"These are a great dessert to serve after a dinner party with a good cup of hot coffee. You can even pre-bake the tart shells and keep them in the freezer until you're ready to use them."
—Grandma Pam

1. Preheat the oven to 350 degrees. Meanwhile, add the cookies to a food processor and pulse until they're coarse crumbs. Then, mix in the melted butter and salt.

2. Form the crushed cookies into mini tart pans and bake them for 12 minutes or until they're just set. Remove them from the oven afterwards and let them cool.

3. For the filling, using a mixer, whip together the cream cheese and powdered sugar until smooth. Then, whip in the chocolate hazelnut spread.

4. Lastly, stream in the heavy cream and vanilla extract and whip until light and fluffy.

5. To serve, dollop some of the filling in each of the tart shells and then drizzle with chocolate sauce.

NOTE: The key to the filling being nice and fluffy is cold ingredients! If the filling doesn't hold too stiff when you whip it after adding the heavy cream, put the bowl in the freezer for 15 minutes, then whip it again. It works like a charm!

RED VELVET CAKE TRIFLE *with vanilla cream cheese frosting*

yield: *Makes 8 servings* | prep time: *15 minutes* | cook time: *18 minutes*

Ingredients

For the red velvet cake
- 2 cups of sugar
- 1 cup of vegetable oil
- 1 1/4 cup of buttermilk
- 2 eggs
- 2 tablespoons of vanilla
- 2 teaspoons of red food coloring
- 1 teaspoon of salt
- 1 teaspoon of baking soda
- 1/2 cup of cocoa powder
- 2 cups of all purpose flour

For the frosting
- 2 8oz packages of cream cheese
- 2 cups of sugar
- 2 teaspoons of vanilla
- 1 cup of very cold heavy cream

"When your cakes don't rise properly or they look bad, but still taste good, use this recipe. Just act like it was your intention all along. Everyone will believe you and they'll be licking their fingers!"

—Grandma Pam

1. Preheat the oven to 350 degrees. In a large bowl, mix together the sugar, vegetable oil, and buttermilk until the sugar has dissolved. Then, add the eggs, red food coloring, and vanilla and mix well until the eggs have been incorporated.

2. Then, add in the salt, baking soda, cocoa powder, and flour and mix until the mixture is smooth. Pour in prepared baking dishes and bake for about 14 minutes or until a toothpick comes out clean once stuck in the center of the cakes.

3. Meanwhile, to make the frosting, using a hand mixer, whip together the cream cheese and sugar until smooth. Then add the vanilla and heavy cream and whip until light and fluffy.

4. After the cakes have cooled, to assemble the trifles, add crumbles of the cake and a dollop or so of frosting alternatively to a dish.

> **NOTE:** The best way to prepare a baking dish for baking a cake is to coat the entire dish with room temperature butter. Then, dust it with flour. Be sure to tap the dish on the counter so all the excess flour is removed. This will ensure that your cakes don't stick.

OLD FASHIONED STRAWBERRY *and banana pudding*

yield: *Makes 6 servings* | prep time: *10 minutes* | cook time: *20 minutes*

Ingredients

- 1 cup of sugar
- 3 eggs, beaten
- 1 pinch of salt
- 2 tablespoons of cornstarch
- 2 cups of milk
- 1/2 cup of heavy cream
- 1 tablespoon of vanilla
- 2 bananas
- 1 cup of sliced strawberries
- buttered flavored cookies

"This is the only old fashioned pudding recipe I use. It comes out perfect each time! One taste and you'll understand why. Just be sure you add the vanilla after the pudding has thickened. If you do it before, you'll never taste it."

—Grandma Pam

1. In a sauce pan, mix together the sugar and eggs until dissolved. Then, mix in the salt, cornstarch, milk, and heavy cream. Slowly bring this mixture to a boil while constantly whisking. One the mixture comes to a boil, it will thicken. Remove from the heat and stir in the vanilla.
2. Pour the mixture into a bowl and allow it to come to room temperature.
3. Layer the pudding with bananas, sliced strawberries, and the cookies. Then, cover tightly and chill the pudding at least 4 hours.
4. To serve, top the pudding with fresh strawberries, bananas, and cookie crumbs.

NOTE: Be sure to continue to whisk while the flame is on low. You don't want to scorch the pan, so take your time with this one. Once the pan is scorched and the milk is burned, then the entire batch becomes no good anymore.

SALTED CARAMEL *shortbread tart*

yield: *Makes 4 servings* | prep time: *10 minutes* | cook time: *12 minutes*

Ingredients

For the shortbread crust
- 1 cup of softened butter
- 1/2 cup of sugar
- 2 cups of flour
- 1 pinch of salt

For the filling
- Store-bought Dulce de leche spread
- 2 cups of shelled pecans
- Kosher salt

"There's nothing better than caramel. When you add salt to it, it turns up the volume. I'm such a fan of semi-homemade desserts that taste like you've worked all day to make them!"
—Grandma Pam

1. Preheat the oven to 350 degrees. To make the crust, mix together the butter, sugar, and salt until combined. Then mix in the flour until the dough is formed. Form the dough into the bottom of a tart pan and bake for 12 minutes until the dough has set.

2. Once the crust has baked, allow it to cool.

3. Meanwhile, arrange the pecans on a sheet tray and bake them in the oven for 6 minutes until they're toasted. Remove from the oven and let them cool down.

4. To assemble the tart, add some Dulce de leche spread to the bottom of the tart. Then arrange the toasted pecans and top with a sprinkle of Kosher salt.

NOTE: Short on time? Pre-bake the crusts and leave them in an air tight container until you're ready to use them. Then, you'll have dessert ready in a cinch.

BUTTERMILK POUND CAKE *with lemon lime glaze*

yield: *Makes 8 servings* | prep time: *15 minutes* | cook time: *40 minutes*

Ingredients

For the pound cake
- 3 cups of flour
- 1/4 teaspoon of baking soda
- 1/2 teaspoon of salt
- 1 1/4 cup of butter, at room temperature
- 6 eggs
- 3 cups of sugar
- 2 teaspoons of vanilla
- 1 cup of buttermilk

For the glaze
- 2 tablespoons of lemon juice
- 2 tablespoons of lime juice
- 2 cups of powdered sugar

"I typically make this cake the day before I want to serve it. Letting it sit overnight allows the moisture to really redistribute itself. If you've got the time, don't skip that step!"

-Grandma Pam

1. Preheat the oven to 325 degrees. In a large bowl, mix together the flour, baking soda, and salt and set aside.
2. Meanwhile, in another bowl, using a mixer, whip the butter and sugar together until light and fluffy. Then, mix in the eggs, one at a time. Next, add the vanilla extract.
3. Lastly, add in the flour and buttermilk alternatively. Pour the batter into a pan that's been buttered well and bake for 35-40 minutes or until a toothpick comes out clean.
4. To make the glaze, pour the powdered sugar into a bowl. Add 1 tablespoon of fruit juice at a time. The glaze should be thick and pourable. Once the cakes have cooled, pour the glaze over the top of the cakes and let them sit for about 5 minutes before cutting.

NOTE: This is such an easy cake recipe, you really can't screw it up. Just remember, it's best to have all of your ingredients at room temperature, even the buttermilk. This way, each ingredient will blend well and your batter will be nice and smooth.

VANILLA BEAN CARROT *cake cheesecake with caramel sauce*

yield: *Makes 8 servings* | prep time: *20 minutes* | cook time: *25 minutes*

Ingredients

For the cheesecake batter
-2 8oz packages of cream cheese, room temperature
-3 cups of sugar
-4 eggs
-2 teaspoons of vanilla
-1 pinch of salt

For the carrot cake batter
-2 cups of sugar
-1 cup of vegetable oil
-1 1/4 cups of buttermilk
-1 tablespoon of vanilla
-1 tablespoon of cinnamon
-2 eggs
-1 teaspoon of salt
-1 cup of shredded carrots
-2 cups of flour
-1 teaspoon of baking soda

For the crust
-1 1/2 cups of graham cracker crumbs
-6 tablespoons of melted butter
-1/3 cup of sugar

-whipped cream, to garnish
-caramel sauce, to garnish

"This cake/cheesecake is addictive. The key to making it perfect is letting it chill for at least 4 hours. I typically do it overnight, this way I know it'll be perfect when I cut into it."

-Grandma Pam

1. Preheat the oven to 350 degrees. For the crust, mix together the graham cracker crumbs, melted butter, and sugar. Form in the bottom of a cake pan and set aside.

2. For the carrot cake batter, mix together the sugar, vegetable oil, and buttermilk until the sugar has dissolved. Then, mix in the eggs and vanilla. Then, mix in the cinnamon, salt, baking soda, and flour. Set aside.

3. For the cheesecake batter, mix together the cream cheese and sugar until well combined. Then, add the eggs one at a time and mix well. Finally, mix in the vanilla and salt. Set aside.

4. To bake the dessert, pour the cheese cake batter in the graham cracker crust first. Then, carefully pour in the carrot cake batter. Bake the mixture for 22-25 minutes or until the cake batter has set. Let come to room temperature. Then, chill for at least 4 hours.

5. To serve, top with whipped cream and a drizzle of caramel sauce.

NOTE: The only way to test if the dessert is ready to come out of the oven is by testing the top layer of cake. Make sure the cake has cooked through by inserting a toothpick in the cake part only. If it comes out clean, you're good to go.

BANANA *pudding cheesecake*

Ingredients

For the crust
- 1 1/2 cups of vanilla wafer cookie crumbs
- 6 tablespoons of melted butter
- 1/3 cup of sugar

For the filling
- 2 8 oz packages of cream cheese, room temperature
- 1 1/3 cup of sugar
- 1 pinch of salt
- 2 teaspoons of vanilla
- 4 eggs
- 2/3 cup of sour cream
- 2 bananas, mashed

For the topping
- 2 cups of heavy cream
- 1/2 cup of sugar
- 1 teaspoon of vanilla
- cookies & bananas, to garnish

"To make your life easier, make this dessert the day before. This way, it's got time to set and chill before you need to garnish it the next day!"
—Grandma Pam

1. Preheat the oven to 350 degrees. For the crust, combine the cookies crumbs, butter, and sugar together. Form the mixture into the bottom of a spring form pan.

2. To make the filling, using a mixer, combine the cream cheese and sugar until smooth. Then, add in the sugar, vanilla, and salt and mix until smooth. Lastly, add the eggs, one egg at a time until combined. Then, using a rubber spatula, fold in the sour cream and mashed bananas.

3. Bake the cheesecake for 25 minutes or just until it's set in the middle. Allow it to come to room temperature, then chill in the refrigerator for at least 4 hours.

4. To make the whipped cream, add the heavy cream, sugar, and vanilla to a bowl. Then, using a mixer, whip until the cream has thickened. Add the cream to the top of the cheesecake and garnish with bananas and cookies.

NOTE: The key is to mash the bananas until they've become a pulp. Then, mix the pulp with the cheesecake batter. Doing this will allow for each bit to have some banana in it and that will make everyone happy!

RED VELVET BROWNIES *with cream cheese frosting*

yield: *Makes 8 servings* | prep time: *10 minutes* | cook time: *15 minutes*

Ingredients

For the brownies
- 1/2 cup of vegetable oil
- 1 cup of sugar
- 1 tablespoon of vanilla
- 2 eggs
- 1/2 teaspoon of baking powder
- 1/2 cup of cocoa powder
- 2 tablespoons of red food coloring
- 1/2 teaspoon of salt
- 1/2 cup of flour

For the frosting
- 1 8oz package of cream cheese
- 1 cup of heavy cream
- 1 cup of sugar
- 1 tablespoon of vanilla

"Red velvet anything is delicious. These brownies are especially delicious because they're light and not too dense. It's a perfect accompaniment to the whipped cream cheese frosting!"
—Grandma Pam

1. Preheat the oven to 350 degrees. In a large bowl, whisk together the vegetable oil, sugar, and eggs.

2. Then, mix in the vanilla, baking powder, cocoa powder, red food coloring, salt, and flour.

3. Pour the brownie batter into a baking dish that's been greased and bake for 15 minutes or until the center of the brownies have just set. Then take the brownies out and let them cool.

4. To make the frosting, whip together the cream cheese and sugar until the sugar has dissolved. Then, pour in the heavy cream and vanilla and whip together until the mixture frosting is light and fluffy. Top the cooled brownies with the frosting and serve.

NOTE: Make sure you butter your baking dish. Then, be sure to dust it with flour and shake out the excess flour. This is your insurance policy that your brownies come out without sticking to the pan.

CHOCOLATE PEANUT BUTTER *shortbread tarts*

yield: *Makes 6 servings* | prep time: *15 minutes* | cook time: *15 minutes*

Ingredients

For the shortbread crust
- 1 cup of softened butter
- 1/2 cup of sugar
- 2 cups of flour
- 1 pinch of salt

For the chocolate ganache
- 2 cups of semi-sweet chocolate chips
- 1 cup of heavy cream
- 1/2 teaspoon of vanilla
- 1 teaspoon of instant coffee granules

For the peanut butter cream
- 1 8oz package of cream cheese
- 2 tablespoons of smooth peanut butter
- 1 cup of sugar
- 1 tablespoon of vanilla
- 2/3 cup of heavy cream

- salted peanuts, to garnish
- chocolate sauce, to garnish

"The best thing about this dessert, besides the taste, is that most of these ingredients are pantry staples. This means this is a super economic-friendly dessert that just happens to also taste amazing!"

-Grandma Pam

1. Preheat the oven to 350 degrees. To make the crust, mix together the butter, sugar, and salt until combined. Then, mix in the flour until the dough is formed. Form the dough into the bottom of a tart pan and bake for 12 minutes until the dough has set.

2. Once the crust has baked, allow it to cool.

3. To make the chocolate ganache, heat the chocolate in the microwave 30 seconds at a time until it's just melted. Then, remove it from the microwave and mix in the vanilla, instant coffee granules, and heavy cream. Mix well until smooth. If necessary, place the ganache back in the microwave for 15 second increments until fully melted and smooth.

4. To make the peanut butter cream, using a mixer, whip together the cream cheese, peanut butter, and sugar until smooth. Then, add in the vanilla and heavy cream and whip until light and fluffy.

5. To assemble the tarts, pour in some of the ganache in the bottom of the shortbread crust. Then, top with peanut butter cream and garnish with salted peanuts and chocolate sauce.

NOTE: All of the components of this dessert can be made ahead of time and then stored properly. Then, when you're ready, just assemble the dessert and serve. Your guests will think you spent all day preparing!

OLD FASHIONED BOURBON *peach cobbler crisps*

yield: *Makes 8 servings* | prep time: *5 minutes* | cook time: *30 minutes*

Ingredients

For the crumble
- 1 stick of butter, room temperature
- 1/2 cup of brown sugar
- 1/2 cup of granulated sugar
- 1 1/2 cups of flour

For the filling
- 4 to 6 cups of sliced peaches
- 1 cup of sugar
- 1/2 cup of brown sugar
- 1 teaspoon of salt
- 1 1/2 teaspoons of cinnamon
- 1/2 teaspoon of allspice
- 3 tablespoons of lemon juice
- 3 tablespoons of corn starch
- 1/2 stick of melted butter
- 1/2 cup of good bourbon

"Crumbles are easy. Just toss some good fruit with great spices and bake in the oven. It's the perfect simple dessert for any time of the year!"

-Grandma Pam

1. Preheat the oven to 350 degrees. For the crumble, add the butter, brown sugar, granulated sugar, and flour to a bowl. Mix well until crumbles form and set aside.

2. Meanwhile, add the peaches to a large bowl. Then, mix in the sugar, brown sugar, salt, cinnamon, allspice, lemon juice, corn starch, butter, and bourbon. Toss well.

3. Pour the filling into an oven safe dish and top the filling with a fair amount of crumble mixture. Bake for 25-30 minutes or until the crumble is golden brown.

NOTE: For the absolute best results, always use fresh or frozen fruit. If you're in an absolute pinch and you must, then use canned.

CHOCOLATE HAZELNUT *pop-tarty pastries*

yield: *Makes 4 servings* | prep time: *15 minutes* | cook time: *12 minutes*

Ingredients

For the pastry
-2 cups of all purpose flour
-1 cup of unsweetened cocoa powder
-1 cup of sugar
-1 1/2 sticks of cold butter, cut into small cubes
-1/2 teaspoon of salt
-4-6 tablespoons of cold water

-flour, for dusting
-4 heaping tablespoons of chocolate hazelnut spread
-chocolate sauce, to garnish
-powdered sugar, to garnish

"These are perfect for a decadent breakfast. They also travel well. Put a few in your purse and when you're out and get the munchies, they'll satisfy your hunger!"

—Grandma Pam

1. Preheat the oven to 350 degrees. To make the dough, in a large bowl, mix together the flour, unsweetened cocoa powder, sugar, and salt until well combined.

2. Then, mix in the butter until it's really incorporated. When the mixture almost holds together when you form it with your fist, then it's ready.

3. Mix in the cold water, one tablespoon at a time, until the dough just forms together. Form it in to a ball and let it rest in the refrigerator for at least an hour. Then, roll the dough out to 1/2 inch thick sheet. Be sure to dust the surface with flour so the dough doesn't stick.

4. Cut the dough into squares. Fill half of the squares with a layer of chocolate hazelnut spread and then cover the filled squares with the remaining squares. Use a fork to crimp the edges of the pastry.

5. Bake in the oven for 10-12 minutes, or just until pastry is cooked through. Allow to cool. To serve, garnish with chocolate sauce and powdered sugar.

NOTE: The key to flaky pastry is to make sure you let it chill in the fridge. When the heat of the oven gets to the butter, the steam escapes. That's what causes super flaky pastry. Don't forget to chill your dough!

CHOCOLATE CHIP *cookie cupcakes*

Ingredients

For the chocolate chip cookies

- 2 1/4 cups of flour
- 1/2 teaspoon of baking soda
- 2 sticks of butter, room temperature
- 1/2 cup of white sugar
- 1 cup of light brown sugar
- 1 teaspoon of salt
- 2 teaspoons of vanilla
- 2 eggs
- 2 cups of semi-sweet chocolate chips

For the cupcakes

- 2 cups of sugar
- 1 cup of vegetable oil
- 1 1/4 cups of buttermilk
- 2 eggs
- 1 tablespoon of vanilla
- 1 teaspoon of salt
- 1 teaspoon of baking soda
- 2 1/4 cups of flour
- 1 1/2 cups of chocolate chip cookie crumbles

For the frosting

- 2 8oz packages of cream cheese
- 1 cup of heavy cream
- 1 1/2 cups of sugar
- 1 tablespoon of vanilla
- 1 cup of chocolate chip cookie crumbles

"These chocolate chip cookies are crispy on the edges and gooey on the inside. They're addictive. Do your best not to devour them before you've added them to the cupcakes!"

—Grandma Pam

1. Preheat the oven to 350 degrees. In a large bowl, mix together the butter, white sugar, and brown sugar until well combined. Then, add in one egg at a time along with the vanilla, and mix well to incorporate.

2. In another bowl, mix together the flour, baking soda, salt. Once well combined, add to the dough and mix well to incorporate. Fold in the chocolate chips. Dollop tablespoon portions of dough onto a cookie sheet and bake for 8-10 minutes, just until they're set on the outside. Remove and let cool.

3. To make the cupcakes, mix the sugar, vegetable oil, and buttermilk together until dissolved. Then, add in the eggs, vanilla, salt, baking soda, and flour and mix until well combined. Fold in the chocolate chip cookie crumbles, pour into cupcake liners, and bake for 12-15 minutes until the cupcakes are set. Remove and let cool.

4. To make the frosting, whip together the cream cheese and sugar until the sugar has dissolved. Then add in the vanilla and heavy cream and whip until light and fluffy. Then, fold in the chocolate chip cookie crumbles.

5. To decorate the cupcakes, top each one with as much frosting as you desire. Then, add a cookie and a drizzle of chocolate sauce to each cupcake.

NOTE: For the best results with the chocolate chip cookies, try not to over bake them. Bake them just until the edges have set and they've turned golden brown. They'll turn out soft in the middle…like a cookie should be.

CHOCOLATE COVERED *lunch room butter cookies*

yield: *Makes 8 servings* | prep time: *10 minutes* | cook time: *15 minutes*

Ingredients

For the cookies
-2 sticks of butter, room temperature
-1/2 teaspoon of salt
-1 tablespoon of vanilla
-3/4 cup of powdered sugar
-2 cups of flour

For the chocolate ganache
-2 cups of semi-chocolate chips
-1 teaspoon of instant coffee granules
-1 cup of heavy cream

"These cookies are wildly addictive. They're crunchy and the crumbly texture makes them perfect for dipping in anything. Do yourself a favor and make an extra batch. One bite and you'll understand why!"

-Grandma Pam

1. Preheat the oven to 350 degrees. To make the cookies, mix tougher the butter and sugar until well combined.
2. Then, add in the vanilla and salt. Then, mix in the flour until the cookie dough just comes together.
3. To bake the cookies, form a golf ball sized amount of dough. Form it into a round ball, then press it on a cookie sheet using your index, middle, and ring fingers to make the indentations, Bake for 8-10 minutes until the cookies are golden brown.
4. To make the chocolate ganache, heat the chocolate in the microwave 30 seconds at a time until it's just melted. Then, remove it from the microwave and mix in the vanilla, instant coffee granules, and heavy cream. Mix well until smooth. If necessary, place the ganache back in the microwave in 15 second increments until fully melted and smooth.
5. To serve, dip part of each cookie in the chocolate ganache and enjoy.

NOTE: Resist the temptation to dive into these cookies as soon as they're out of the oven. Let them sit at room temperature for about 30 minutes, first. They're going to get crumbly. This is exactly what you want!

PEACH COBBLER SHORTCAKES *with whipped mascarpone cheese*

yield: *Makes 10 servings* | prep time: *10 minutes* | cook time: *25 minutes*

Ingredients

-1 can of refrigerator biscuits
-2 tablespoons of heavy cream
-2 tablespoons of sugar

For the filling
-2 cups of frozen peaches
-1 cup of white sugar
-1 cup of brown sugar
-2 tablespoon of lemon juice
-1 teaspoon of vanilla
-1 tablespoon of cinnamon
-1 tablespoon of cornstarch
-1 tablespoon of water
-2 tablespoons of butter

For the mascarpone cheese
-1 cup of mascarpone cheese
-1/2 cup of heavy cream
-2 teaspoons of vanilla
-1/2 cup of sugar

"Refrigerator biscuits aren't just for breakfast. When that's all you've got laying around, you've got to figure out how to get creative. This recipe is a perfect vehicle for that creativity!"
—Grandma Pam

1. Preheat the oven to 350 degrees. Arrange the biscuits on a sheet tray. Brush each biscuit with heavy cream and then sprinkle them with sugar. Bake the biscuits until they're golden brown. Remove and let cool.

2. For the filling, melt the butter in a pan. Add the peaches, sugars, and cinnamon. Cook for about 7-8 minutes until the sugars are completely dissolved. Then, add the lemon juice and vanilla.

3. In another bowl, mix together the water and cornstarch. Once the peach cobbler filling has come to a boil, add the cornstarch mixture and reduce the heat. It will thicken immediately.

4. To make the whipped mascarpone cheese, using a mixer, whip the sugar and mascarpone cheese together until the sugar has dissolved. Then, pour in the vanilla and heavy cream and whip until light and fluffy.

5. To serve, split open the biscuits. Add some of the peach cobbler filling and top with the whipped mascarpone cheese.

NOTE: If you have extra filling leftover, it's great on toast, on top of cereal, yogurt, or even ice cream!

SALTED CARAMEL *banana pudding*

yield: *Makes 8 servings* | prep time: *10 minutes* | cook time: *there is no cook time!*

Ingredients

-1 package of French vanilla
instant pudding
-1 1/2 cups of cold milk
-1 can of sweetened
condensed milk
-2 cups of heavy cream
-4 ripe bananas
-2 cups of your favorite vanilla
flavored cookies

For the salted caramel sauce
-2 cups of granulated sugar
-12 tablespoons of butter,
room temperature
-1 cup of heavy cream
-1 teaspoon of vanilla
-1 tablespoon of flaky sea salt

"There are a lot of shortcuts with this recipe. The addition of the salted caramel sauce turn up the volume and makes this dessert elegant enough for any occasion!"

-Grandma Pam

1. In a large bowl, mix together the instant pudding and the milk. Once mixed, add the sweetened condensed milk, mix well and let stand.

2. In another bowl, whip the heavy cream until it's light and fluffy. Then, using a spatula, fold the whipped cream into the pudding mixture.

3. Layer the cookies, bananas, and pudding mixture in a serving bowl and refrigerate until you're ready to serve.

4. Meanwhile, for the caramel sauce, heat together the sugar and butter on medium heat, until the mixture has turned a brown caramel color. Be sure to stir often to prevent sticking or burning.

5. Then, remove the caramel from the heat and stir in the heavy cream, vanilla, and sea salt. Let cool and then to serve, pour the caramel sauce over the banana pudding. Garnish with more sea salt, if desired.

NOTE: Making caramel from scratch is a wonderful experience. It will smell amazing and the end result will taste even better. Be careful when you add the heavy cream. It will bubble violently, so be prepared!

CHOCOLATE CHIP *cookie dough brownies*

yield: *Makes 9 servings* | prep time: *10 minutes* | cook time: *15 minutes*

Ingredients

For the brownies
- 1/2 cup of vegetable oil
- 1 cup of sugar
- 1 tablespoon of vanilla
- 2 eggs
- 1/2 teaspoon of baking powder
- 1/2 cup of cocoa powder
- 1/2 teaspoon of salt
- 1/2 cup of flour

For the cookie dough filling:
- 1 stick of butter, room temperature
- 1 cup of brown sugar
- 3/4 cup of white sugar
- 1 pinch of salt
- 1 teaspoon of vanilla
- 8 ounces of cream cheese, room temperature
- 3/4 cup of semisweet chocolate chips

For the chocolate ganache
- 2 cups of semi-chocolate chips
- 1 teaspoon of instant coffee granules
- 1 cup of heavy cream
- 1 teaspoon of vanilla

"These are wildly addictive. If you need to stretch them, cut them into small bite sized pieces. Now, you've got enough for everybody. This is also a good way to ensure portion control!"

—Grandma Pam

1. Preheat the oven to 350 degrees. To make the brownies, mix together the vegetable oil, sugar, and eggs until well combined. Then, add in the vanilla, cocoa powder, baking powder, salt, and flour. Pour the batter into a greased baking dish and bake for 13-15 minutes or until the center has set.

2. Meanwhile, to make the cookie dough filling, mix together the cream cheese, butter, and sugar until well combined. Then, add in the salt, and vanilla. Lastly, fold in the chocolate chips until well combined.

3. To make the chocolate ganache, heat the chocolate in the microwave 30 seconds at a time until it's just melted. Then, remove it from the microwave and mix in the vanilla, instant coffee granules, and heavy cream. Mix well until smooth. If necessary, place the ganache back in the microwave in 15 second increments until fully melted and smooth.

4. To assemble the brownies, once they've cooled, top them with the cookie dough filling. Then, top the cookie dough with a layer of chocolate ganache and refrigerate for at least 1 hour.

5. Cut into squares and enjoy.

NOTE: Be sure you've allowed time to let the brownies set and chill in the refrigerator before cutting into them. This will ensure each cut is nice and accurate. If not, you'll have a mess on your hands.

ULTIMATE CHOCOLATE *cupcakes with chocolate hazelnut fulling*

yield: *Makes 24 servings* | prep time: *30 minutes* | cook time: *15 minutes*

Ingredients

For the cupcakes
-2 cups of sugar
-1 cup of vegetable oil
-1 1/2 cups of buttermilk
-1 1/2 tablespoon of vanilla
-2 eggs
-1 pinch of salt
-1 teaspoon of baking soda
-2 cups of flour
-3/4 cup of unsweetened cocoa powder

For the chocolate ganache
-2 cups of semi-chocolate chips
-1 teaspoon of instant coffee granules
-1 cup of heavy cream
-1 teaspoon of vanilla

For the frosting
-2 8oz packs of cream cheese, chilled
-2 cups of sugar
-3/4 cup of unsweetened cocoa powder
-2 cups of cold heavy cream

-brownies, to garnish (from previous page)
-chocolate chips, to garnish
-chocolate hazelnut spread

"If you need a chocolate fix, this one will do it for you. It's super rich, but it's also light. It's chocolatey without being overbearing. And believe it or not, it's not a super sweet cupcake. It's perfect!"
-Grandma Pam

1. Preheat the oven to 350 degrees. To make the cupcakes, mix together the sugar, vegetable oil, and buttermilk until the sugar has dissolved. Then, mix in the vanilla and eggs until well combined. Lastly, add the baking soda, salt, flour, and cocoa powder and mix until well combined. Pour into cupcake liners and bake for 12-15 minutes or until the center is set completely.
2. To make the chocolate ganache, heat the chocolate in the microwave 30 seconds at a time until it's just melted. Then, remove it from the microwave and mix in the vanilla, instant coffee granules, and heavy cream. Mix well until smooth. If necessary, place the ganache back in the microwave in 15 second increments until fully melted and smooth.
3. For the frosting, whip together the cream cheese and sugar until the sugar has dissolved completely. Then add in the unsweetened cocoa powder and heavy cream and whip until light and fluffy.
4. To assemble the cupcakes, use a small knife and put a hole in the center of the cupcakes. Fill it with the chocolate hazelnut spread and then dip the top of the cupcakes into the chocolate ganache. Chill the cupcakes in the refrigerator for at least 20 minutes so the chocolate sets.
5. Lastly, top each cupcake with frosting, a sprinkle of chocolate chips, and a small square of brownie on top.

NOTE: The key for the perfect frosting is to make sure the cream cheese is cold. It will be difficult to whip together at first. But, you'll need the cold temperature to whip the cream perfectly!

CARAMEL AND BANANA TARTS

yield: *Makes 8 servings* | prep time: *20 minutes* | cook time: *10 minutes*

Ingredients

For the crust
- 1 1/2 cups of graham cracker crumbs
- 6 tablespoons of melted butter
- 1/3 cup of sugar

For the caramel filling
- 2 8oz packages of cream cheese
- 2 cups of dark brown sugar
- 1 tablespoon of vanilla
- 1 1/2 cups of heavy cream

For the whipped cream
- 2 cups of heavy cream
- 1 cup of sugar
- 1 tablespoon of vanilla

- sliced bananas, to garnish
- mint, to garnish
- caramel sauce, to garnish

"When there's a lot of homemade going into a recipe, I don't mind using a few store-bought shortcuts. Store-bought caramel sauce is something I always keep on hand to jazz up a dessert!"
-Grandma Pam

1. Preheat the oven to 350 degrees. To make the crust, mix the graham cracker crumbs with the melted butter and sugar. Then, press into a tart pan and bake for 8-10 minutes until lightly golden brown. Remove from the oven and let cool.

2. To make the filling, in a large bowl, mix together the cream cheese and brown sugar until smooth. Then, add the vanilla and heavy cream and whip until light and fluffy.

3. Meanwhile, to make the whipped cream, add the cream, sugar, and vanilla to a bowl and whip until light and fluffy.

4. To assemble the tarts, add the caramel filling to the bottom of the crust, then top with whipped cream. Refrigerate until you're ready to decorate. To decorate, add sliced bananas, a drizzle of caramel sauce, and fresh mint.

NOTE: These tarts are a total do-ahead. Just prep the crusts, filling, and whipped cream and store them separately. When you're ready, just follow step #4 to decorate the tarts!

SOCK-IT-ME CAKE *with buttermilk glaze*

yield: *Makes 8 servings* | prep time: *20 minutes* | cook time: *30 minutes*

Ingredients

For the cake
- 1 cup of vegetable oil
- 1 1/2 cups of buttermilk
- 2 cups of sugar
- 2 eggs
- 1 tablespoon of vanilla
- 1 teaspoon of salt
- 1 teaspoon of baking soda
- 3 cups of flour

For the filling
- 1 1/2 cups of dark brown sugar
- 2 tablespoons of cinnamon
- 1 cup of chopped pecans

For the glaze
- 2 cups of powdered sugar
- 2-3 tablespoons of buttermilk
- 1/2 teaspoon of vanilla

"This cake will make your house smell insanely delicious. The cake is great for eating any time. However, if you heat it in the microwave for just a few seconds, it goes great with a cup of coffee or tea in the morning!"

-Grandma Pam

1. Preheat the oven to 350 degrees. In a large bowl, mix together the oil, buttermilk, and sugar until the sugar has been dissolved. Mix in the eggs and vanilla until well combined. Lastly, stir in the salt, baking soda, and flour until well combined.

2. To prepare the filling, combine the brown sugar, cinnamon, and pecans together in a bowl.

3. In a bundt pan that's been buttered and floured, pour in half the cake batter. Sprinkle the filling mixture on top of the cake batter, then pour on the remaining cake batter. Bake in the oven for 25-30 minutes or until an inserted toothpick comes out clean.

4. While the cake cools, make the glaze by mixing the powdered sugar and vanilla in a bowl. Then, add one tablespoon of buttermilk at at time until the desired consistency is reached.

5. Once the cake has completely cooled, drizzle the glaze all over the cake.

NOTE: For the best results, after the cake cools, let it sit overnight. I know this might be difficult to do. However, once the cake has a chance to sit and rest, it becomes super moist!

Mrs. Fannie – The Cake Goddess

Summers in Chicago are particularly amazing. There is something about the rich-scented Lake Michigan wind that engulfs your senses. The air is calm and as it hits your skin, it offers a refreshing moment of solitude in the middle of a busy day. After church on Sunday mornings, the place to be was the parking lot of our local church. Kids, in their pastels and lace, were running around as free as tumbleweed in the desert heat. The elderly would make their way to their cars, sometimes being accompanied by a deacon or young adult. Women were busy hugging and catching up on the latest news and one by one, you heard and saw people say their goodbyes. If we were lucky, there'd be a church bake sale going on to help raise money for one of the many ministries of the church.

There was always one person's desert we could count on, Mrs. Fannie. She baked cakes. Where I come from, if you could bake a good cake, you were revered. It was like you had a secret power that no one else had. Mrs. Fannie's cakes were particularly delicious. Cakes had to be moist and her cakes were. The frosting was sweet, but not too sweet. The cake layers weren't dense and they weren't light, they had the perfect balance. The cake was so moist, that it would crumb just right as you slid your fork in between the layers of cake. The frosting would lay perfect. As you pulled some of the cake away on your fork, the frosting would follow introducing the perfect cake to frosting ratio. The cakes had some give to them. That meant if you touched it with your index finger, it would spring back at you a bit. That's how you knew the cakes were moist.

Mrs. Fannie's cakes were perfect for eating after your meal has digested. You really wanted to enjoy them, savor them even. My grandmother would say, "Give your food time to digest, then you can have a slice of cake." The anticipation would kill me. We would bring home slices of cake and they'd be wrapped in aluminum foil. Black folks will wrap anything in aluminum foil. It didn't matter if some of the luscious frosting was stuck to the top of the foil. You instinctively knew to just lick it off. To this day, Mrs. Fannie still makes cakes. She is still revered. And, that cake to frosting ratio is still the perfect bite!

eld: *Makes 24 servings* | prep time: *30 minutes* | cook time: *15 minutes*

Ingredients

For the cupcakes

- 1 cup of vegetable oil
- 1 1/2 cups of buttermilk
- 2 cups of sugar
- 2 eggs
- 1 tablespoon of vanilla
- 1/2 teaspoon of salt
- 1 teaspoon of baking soda
- 2 cups of flour
- 1 1/2 cups of cream-filled chocolate wafer cookie crumbs

For the frosting

- 2 8oz packages of cream cheese, cold
- 2 cups of sugar
- 2 cups of heavy cream
- 1 tablespoon of vanilla
- 2 cups of cream-filled chocolate wafer cookie crumbs

"If you can't find the cookie crumbs in your market, no worries. Add cookies to a food storage bag and use the bottom of a cast iron skillet to beat the cookies until they're crumbs. It'll work just the same!"

—Grandma Pam

1. Preheat the oven to 350 degrees. Mix together the vegetable oil, buttermilk, and sugar until the sugar has dissolved. Then, mix in the eggs and vanilla. Lastly, add the salt, baking soda, flour, and cookie crumbs until well mixed.

2. Pour the batter into cupcake liners and bake for 12-15 minutes or until the cupcakes have set in the middle.

3. For the frosting, mix together the cream cheese and sugar until the sugar has dissolved. Then, add in the vanilla and heavy cream and whip until light and fluffy. Lastly, fold in the cream-filled chocolate wafer cookies.

4. To decorate, add the frosting to the top of the cupcakes and and add a cream-filled chocolate wafer cookie to each cupcake.

NOTE: For a nice variation, try using different types of cookies. The cream-filled chocolate wafer cookies look great mixed into the batter and frosting. However, there are a ton of varieties you could use.

RED VELVET CAKE *with cream cheese frosting*

ield: *Makes 10 servings* | prep time: *15 minutes* | cook time: *20 minutes*

Ingredients

For the cake
-2 cups of sugar
-1 cup of vegetable oil
-1 1/4 cups of buttermilk
-2 eggs
-2 teaspoons of vanilla
-2 teaspoons of red food coloring
-1/2 teaspoon of salt
-1 teaspoon of baking soda
-2 cups of flour
-3/4 cup of unsweetened cocoa powder

For the frosting
-2 8oz packages of cream cheese, cold
-2 cups of sugar
-2 tablespoons of vanilla
-1 1/2 cup of heavy cream

"There really is no other red velvet cake recipe that you'll need other than this one. The whipped cream cheese frosting paired with the moist cake makes the perfect bite!"
-Grandma Pam

1. Preheat the oven to 350 degrees. For the cake, mix together the sugar, vegetable oil, and buttermilk until the sugar dissolves. Then, add in the eggs, vanilla, and red food coloring and mix together until well combined. Lastly, add the salt, baking soda, flour, and cocoa powder and mix well.

2. Pour the batter into two 9-inch round baking pans that have been buttered and floured. Bake for 17-20 minutes or until the center is set.

3. Meanwhile, for the frosting, whip together the cream cheese and sugar until the sugar has dissolved. Then, add in the vanilla and heavy cream and whip until light and fluffy.

4. Once the cakes have come out of the oven, allow them to cool completely. Then, frost the cake with the cream cheese frosting and enjoy.

NOTE: For the best results, make the cakes a day ahead of time. Then, let them cool on a counter over night. The next day, they'll be super moist!

recipe index

Anchovy Paste	Chicken & Waffle Caesar Salad	59
Apple, Green	Crispy Pork Belly with Whipped Feta & Green Apple Salsa	16
Artichokes	Collard Green & Artichoke Fondue	35
Artichokes	Spinach & Artichoke Risotto	74
Artichokes	Spinach & Artichoke Stuffed Shrimp	41
Artichokes	Spinach & Artichoke Twice Baked Potatoes	91
Asparagus	Prosciutto Wrapped Asparagus with Balsamic Glaze	39
Bacon	Chicken Fried Shrimp with Corn & Bacon Gravy	130
Bacon	Grandma Pam's Fried Sweet Corn	72
Bacon	Shrimp & Grits with Bacon Butter	141
Bacon	Winter Succotach with Bacon	97
Bananas	Banana Pudding Cheesecake	198
Bananas	Caramel & Banana Tarts	222
Bananas	Old Fashioned Strawberry & Banana Pudding	190
Beans, Green	Sauteed Green Beans with Crispy Potatoes	85
Beans, Lima	Winter Succotach with Bacon	97
Beans, Red Kidney	New Orleans Style Red Beans & Rice	57
Beans, White	My Mama's Skillet Chicken with White Bean Puree	170
Beef, Short Ribs	6-Hour Wine Braised Short Ribs	172
Beef, Short Ribs	Slow Cooker Short Rib & Sweet Potato Stew	65
Biscuits	Chicken & Biscuits on a Stick with Sausage & Herb Gravy	28
Bourbon	Old Fashioned Bourbon Peach Cobbler Crisps	205
Brussels Sprouts	Balsamic & Honey Roasted Brussels Sprouts	102
Butter	Chocolate Covered Lunchroom Butter Cookies	212
Cabbage	Chili Garlic Cabbage	87
Capers	Brown Sugar Rubbed Salmon with Black Olive Tapenade	151
Capers	Crispy Chicken with Lime Caper Sauce	125
Capers	Puttanesca Chicken Fettuccine	183
Caramel	Caramel & Banana Tarts	222
Caramel	Vanilla Bean Carrot Cake Cheese Cake with Caramel Sauce	196
Caramel, Salted	Salted Caramel Banana Pudding	216
Carrots	Smothered Chicken Pot Pie	149
Carrots	Vanilla Bean Carrot Cake Cheese Cake with Caramel Sauce	196
Catfish	Pecan Crusted Catfish	161
Cheese, Cheddar	Chicken Sausage Breakfast Hash-lettes	135
Cheese, Cheddar	Double Cheddar Ox-Tail Sandwich with Sweet Lime Slaw	137
Cheese, Cheddar	Pea & Cheddar Salad with Cajun Grilled Shrimp	61
Cheese, Cheddar	The Ultimate Baked Mac & Cheese	109
Cheese, Cream	Banana Pudding Cheesecake	198
Cheese, Cream	Caramel & Banana Tarts	222
Cheese, Cream	Chocolate Chip Cookie Cupcakes	209
Cheese, Cream	Chocolate Chip Cookie Dough Brownies	218
Cheese, Cream	Chocolate Hazelnut Mini Tarts	186
Cheese, Cream	Chocolate Peanutbutter Shortbread Tarts	202
Cheese, Cream	Cookies & Cream Cupcakes with Cookies & Cream Frosting	227
Cheese, Cream	Red Velvet Brownies with Cream Cheese Frosting	200
Cheese, Cream	Red Velvet Cake Trifle	188
Cheese, Cream	Red Velvet Cake with Cream Cheese Frosting	229
Cheese, Cream	Ultimate Chocolate Cupcakes with Chocolate Hazelnut Filling	220
Cheese, Cream	Vanilla Bean Carrot Cake Cheese Cake with Caramel Sauce	196
Cheese, Fontina	The Ultimate Baked Mac & Cheese	109
Cheese, Gouda	The Ultimate Baked Mac & Cheese	109
Cheese, Mascarpone	Peach Cobbler Shortcakes with Whipped Mascarpone Cheese	214
Cheese, Mascarpone	Spinach & Artichoke Risotto	74
Cheese, Mascarpone	Spinach & Artichoke Twice Baked Potatoes	91
Cheese, Mozzarella	Crispy Grilled Cheese Won-Tons	21
Cheese, Parmesan	Braised Collard Green Fettuccine with Smoked Turkey	178
Cheese, Parmesan	Chicken & Waffle Caesar Salad	59
Cheese, Parmesan	Collard Green Pesto Roasted Tomatoes	100
Cheese, Parmesan	Creamed Field Greens with French Fried Onions	113
Cheese, Parmesan	Spinach & Artichoke Risotto	74
Cheese, Parmesan	Spinach & Artichoke Stuffed Shrimp	41
Cheese, White Cheddar	Collard Green & Artichoke Fondue	35
Cheese, White Cheddar	Mini Ham, Cheese, and Potato Tarts	43
Cheese, White Cheddar	Spinach & Artichoke Twice Baked Potatoes	91
Cheese, White Cheddar	White Cheddar & Garlic Scalloped Potatoes	93
Chicken, Breasts	Chicken & Biscuits on a Stick with Sausage & Herb Gravy	28
Chicken, Breasts	Crispy Chicken with Lime Caper Sauce	125
Chicken, Breasts	French Fry Crusted Chicken Strips	50
Chicken, Breasts	Pulled Jerk Chicken Sliders	163

Chicken, Breasts	Scampi Grilled Chicken Bites	48
Chicken, Fried	Cornbread Cupcakes with Mashed Potato Frosting	31
Chicken, Ground	Chicken & Waffle Fritters	18
Chicken, Ground	Chicken Meatballs with Sweet Red Sauce	37
Chicken, Ground	Chicken Meatloaf with Tomato Ketchup Glaze	157
Chicken, Ground	Chicken Sausage Breakfast Hash-lettes	135
Chicken, Leftover	Puttanesca Chicken Fettuccine	183
Chicken, Thighs	Smothered Chicken Pot Pie	149
Chicken, Whole	Garlic & Herb Roast Chicken with Roasted Root Vegetables	127
Chicken, Whole	My Granny's Brown Bag Fried Chicken	143
Chicken, Whole	My Mama's Skillet Chicken with White Bean Puree	170
Chicken, Whole	Rainbow Candy Glazed Chicken	176
Chicken, Wings	Jerk Fried Chicken	133
Chicken, Wings	Peach Balsamic Glazed Wings	121
Chicken, Wings	Sriracha Glazed Chicken Wings	123
Chipotle	Chorizo Burger with Sauteed Shrimp & Chipotle Mayo	153
Cookie Crumbles	Chocolate Chip Cookie Cupcakes	209
Chocolate Hazelnut Spread	Chocolate Hazelnut Mini Tarts	186
Chocolate Hazelnut Spread	Chocolate Hazelnut Pop-Tarty Pastries	207
Chocolate Hazelnut Spread	Ultimate Chocolate Cupcakes with Chocolate Hazelnut Filling	220
Chorizo	Chorizo Burger with Sauteed Shrimp & Chipotle Mayo	153
Coconut Milk	Coconut Yam Rice	82
Corn	Chicken Fried Shrimp with Corn & Bacon Gravy	130
Corn	Grandma Pam's Fried Sweet Corn	72
Corn	Grilled Corn On The Cob with Honey Butter	89
Corn	Winter Succotach with Bacon	97
Cornbread	Collard Green & Cornbread Cake	159
Cornbread	Cornbread Cupcakes with Mashed Potato Frosting	31
Cornbread	Southern Style Sausage & Cornbread Dressing	117
Cranberry	Cranberry & Orange Relish	33
Cucumbers, English	English Cucumber Salad with Balsamic Dressing	63
Dill	Roasted Potatoes with Dill Chimichurri	80
Feta Cheese	Crispy Pork Belly with Whipped Feta & Green Apple Salsa	16
Fettuccine	Braised Collard Green Fettuccine with Smoked Turkey	178
Greens, Collards	Braised Collard Green Fettuccine with Smoked Turkey	178

Greens, Collards	Collard Green & Artichoke Fondue	35
Greens, Collards	Collard Green & Cornbread Cake	159
Greens, Collards	Collard Green Pesto Roasted Tomatoes	100
Greens, Collards	Spicy Braised Collard Greens with Smoked Turkey	70
Greens, Collards	Stewed Greems & Tomatoes	105
Grits	6-Hour Wine Braised Short Ribs	172
Ham	Mini Ham, Cheese, and Potato Tarts	43
Honey	Balsamic & Honey Roasted Brussels Sprouts	102
Honey	Butter Pecan Cornbread with Honey Butter	46
Honey	Grilled Corn On The Cob with Honey Butter	89
Jerk BBQ Sauce	Pulled Jerk Chicken Sliders	163
Jerk Spice Rub	Jerk Fried Chicken	133
Lemon	Brown Sugar Rubbed Salmon with Black Olive Tapenade	151
Lemon	Buttermilk Pound Cake with Lemon Lime Glaze	194
Lemon	Chicken & Waffle Caesar Salad	59
Lemon	Lemon & Garlic Pork Chops	139
Lemon	Old Fashioned Bourbon Peach Cobbler Crisps	205
Lemon	Scampi Grilled Chicken Bites	48
Lettuce, Romaine	Chicken & Waffle Caesar Salad	59
Lime	Buttermilk Pound Cake with Lemon Lime Glaze	194
Lime	Crispy Chicken with Lime Caper Sauce	125
Lime	Crispy Okra with Chili-Lime Salt	77
Lime	Double Cheddar Ox-Tail Sandwich with Sweet Lime Slaw	137
Lime	Steak Fajita Pitas	180
Okra	Crispy Okra with Chili-Lime Salt	77
Olives, Black	Brown Sugar Rubbed Salmon with Black Olive Tapenade	151
Olives, Black	Puttanesca Chicken Fettuccine	183
Orange	Cranberry & Orange Relish	33
Oxtails	Double Cheddar Ox-Tail Sandwich with Sweet Lime Slaw	137
Panko Breadcrumbs	Spinach & Artichoke Stuffed Shrimp	41
Peaches	Old Fashioned Bourbon Peach Cobbler Crisps	205
Peaches	Peach Balsamic Glazed Wings	121
Peaches	Peach Cobbler Shortcakes with Whipped Mascarpone Cheese	214
Peanut Butter	Chocolate Peanutbutter Shortbread Tarts	202
Peas	Pea & Cheddar Salad with Cajun Grilled Shrimp	61

Peas, Black Eyed	Winter Succotach with Bacon	97
Peas, Green	Smothered Chicken Pot Pie	149
Pecans	Butter Pecan Cornbread with Honey Butter	46
Pecans	Collard Green Pesto Roasted Tomatoes	100
Pecans	Crispy Pecan Crusted Shrimp	174
Pecans	Pecan Crusted Catfish	161
Pecans	Salted Caramel Shortbread Tart	192
Pecans	Sock-It-To-Me Cake with Buttermilk Glaze	224
Pork Belly	Crispy Pork Belly with Whipped Feta & Green Apple Salsa	16
Pork Chops	Cornmeal Crusted Pork Chops	155
Pork Chops	Lemon & Garlic Pork Chops	139
Potatoes, Mashed	Cornbread Cupcakes with Mashed Potato Frosting	31
Potatoes, Russet	Southern Style Potato Salad	55
Potatoes, Russet	Spinach & Artichoke Twice Baked Potatoes	91
Potatoes, Russet	White Cheddar & Garlic Scalloped Potatoes	93
Potatoes, Sweet	6-Hour Wine Braised Short Ribs	172
Potatoes, Sweet	Coconut Yam Rice	82
Potatoes, Sweet	Slow Cooker Short Rib & Sweet Potato Stew	65
Potatoes, Sweet	Whipped Sweet Potatoes with Salt	111
Potatoes, Yukon	Mini Ham, Cheese, and Potato Tarts	43
Prosciutto	Prosciutto Wrapped Asparagus with Balsamic Glaze	39
Rice	Coconut Yam Rice	82
Rice	Roasted Veggie Rice Pilaf	115
Rice	Spinach & Artichoke Risotto	74
Salmon	Brown Sugar Rubbed Salmon with Black Olive Tapenade	151
Sausage	Chicken & Biscuits on a Stick with Sausage & Herb Gravy	28
Sausage	Southern Style Sausage & Cornbread Dressing	117
Shrimp	Chicken Fried Shrimp with Corn & Bacon Gravy	130
Shrimp	Chorizo Burger with Sauteed Shrimp & Chipotle Mayo	153
Shrimp	Crispy Pecan Crusted Shrimp	174
Shrimp	Pea & Cheddar Salad with Cajun Grilled Shrimp	61
Shrimp	Shrimp & Grits with Bacon Butter	141
Shrimp	Spinach & Artichoke Stuffed Shrimp	41
Sour Cream	The Ultimate Baked Mac & Cheese	109
Spinach	Spinach & Artichoke Risotto	74

Spinach	Spinach & Artichoke Stuffed Shrimp	41
Spinach	Spinach & Artichoke Twice Baked Potatoes	91
Sriracha	Sriracha Glazed Chicken Wings	123
Steak, Cube	Smothered Cube Steak with Garlic Mashed Potatoes	145
Steak, Rib Eye	Steak Fajita Pitas	180
Strawberries	Old Fashioned Strawberry & Banana Pudding	190
Tomateos, Cherry	Collard Green Pesto Roasted Tomatoes	100
Tomatoes, Canned	Chicken Meatballs with Sweet Red Sauce	37
Turkey, Breast	Chicken Fried Turkey with Cornbread Waffles	166
Turkey, Smoked	Braised Collard Green Fettuccine with Smoked Turkey	178
Turkey, Tail	New Orleans Style Red Beans & Rice	57
Turkey, Tail	Spicy Braised Collard Greens with Smoked Turkey	70
Turkey, Wing	New Orleans Style Red Beans & Rice	57
Turkey, Wing	Spicy Braised Collard Greens with Smoked Turkey	70
Turkey, Wing	Stewed Greems & Tomatoes	105
Vinegar, Apple Cider	Chili Garlic Cabbage	87
Vinegar, Apple Cider	Pea & Cheddar Salad with Cajun Grilled Shrimp	61
Vinegar, Apple Cider	Roasted Potatoes with Dill Chimichurri	80
Vinegar, Apple Cider	Southern Style Potato Salad	55
Vinegar, Balsamic	Balsamic & Honey Roasted Brussels Sprouts	102
Vinegar, Balsamic	English Cucumber Salad with Balsamic Dressing	63
Vinegar, Balsamic	Peach Balsamic Glazed Wings	121
Vinegar, Balsamic	Prosciutto Wrapped Asparagus with Balsamic Glaze	39
Waffles	Chicken Fried Turkey with Cornbread Waffles	166
Wine, Red	6-Hour Wine Braised Short Ribs	172
Wine, Red	Slow Cooker Short Rib & Sweet Potato Stew	65
Wine, White	Braised Collard Green Fettuccine with Smoked Turkey	178
Wine, White	Crispy Chicken with Lime Caper Sauce	125
Wine, White	Crispy Pork Belly with Whipped Feta & Green Apple Salsa	16
Wine, White	Garlic & Herb Roast Chicken with Roasted Root Vegetables	127
Wine, White	Scampi Grilled Chicken Bites	48
Wine, White	Spinach & Artichoke Risotto	74
Wine, White	Winter Succotach with Bacon	97
Won-ton Wrappers	Crispy Grilled Cheese Won-Tons	21

"Stories from My Grandmother's Kitchen" is a collection of recipes and stories rooted deep within the bends and curves of the Mississippi River. You'll enjoy over 100 original recipes. Each recipe has a delicious photo so you know how the finished dish is supposed to look. Additionally, the author, Darius Williams, recalls many great stories from his childhood that helped shape his culinary point of view. The book is organized into 4 sections. "Snacks, Appetizers, and Whatnots" features creative recipes like Crispy Grilled Cheese Won-Tons and Chicken & Waffle Fritters. "Side Dishes" speak one language - the language of comfort! This section features recipes like The Ultimate Baked Mac & Cheese and Creamed Field Greens with French Fried Onions. You'll salivate over the "Meats, Seafood, and Main Dishes" section of the book with recipes like the Collard Green & Cornbread Cake and the Chorizo Burger with Sautéed Shrimp and Chipotle Mayo. This book holds no punches on dessert! The "Desserts & All Things Sweet" section features amazing recipes like Chocolate Covered Lunchroom Butter Cookies and Salted Caramel Banana Pudding. Whether you're a novice in the kitchen or a professional chef, the recipes in this book will speak to you. The recipes will take you on a journey, just like a good story. This is a must for your collection!

Collard Green & Cornbread Cake - Page 159

Salted Caramel Banana Pudding - Page 215

Chorizo Burger with Shrimp - Page 152

Darius Williams, Author

"Food is my life. Life is my food!"

www.DariusCooks.com

$32.99
ISBN 978-0-9963478-0-8

9 780996 347808